LEADer

MORAL ATTRIBUTES OF A KINGDOM LEADER

Vincent Robinson

LEADer

MORAL ATTRIBUTES OF A KINGDOM LEADER

LEADer

Moral Attributes of a Kingdom LEADer

Copyright © 2022 by Vincent Robinson
ISBN: 978-1-7360064-5-0
Published by Robinson Media and Publishing Mobile, AL
www.vrministries.org www.rightwayccc.org

Subjects: Empowerment | Leadership | Motivation

Table of Content

Acknowledgement

I want to dedicate this book to my team. To the amazing staff and department LEADs at Right Way Christian Center. I count it a privilege and an honour to serve alongside each of you. You capture the vision, give input, and continue to run with it. Your contribution to Right Way has caused us to live out our vision, meet every goal set forth, and demonstrate the love of God to the community and city.

Thank you for your support, love, and continuing motivation to be and do better.

Right Place, Right Time, Right Way
Dr.V

"A man is better kept by character and integrity than by gift, strategy, and talent alone."

Dr. Vincent Robinson

Introduction
LEADership Matters

" What we need today more
than anything is LEADership "

The vast majority of our training and LEADership books today provide information on how to lead others effectively. Books with systems, techniques, tools, and structures that show the person LEADing the how-tos, and a plethora of books that we can find that deal with effectively LEADing others. But there are very few books for LEADers on the importance of LEADing themselves. Books that are intentional about holding the one who's LEADing accountable.

There are too many Kingdom LEADers failing. And although we are mere men, the good that we achieve and the messages we teach, though true in themselves, become tainted when we are a reproach to the very things we are teaching. Jesus gives a grave warning to the LEADer who causes His children to stumble: *But whoever causes one of these little ones who believe in and acknowledge and cleave to me to stumble and sin [that is, who entices him or hinders him in right conduct or thought], it would be better (more expedient and profitable or advantageous) for him to have a great millstone fastened around his neck and to be sunk in the depth of the sea* (Matthew 18:6 AMPC). We not only have a responsibility to the flock given to us or the people we have been assigned to lead, but we have been given the responsibility of taking heed to ourselves also (Acts 20:28). There are numerous warnings to LEADers about the grave losses from immoral acts, selfish ambitions, and mistreatment of people. Still, if the LEADer is not intentional about holding themselves to a godly standard, no warning will keep them from entering into contempt. We should be desirous of God's power flowing through us, but even more desirous of His power working in us as well.

I believe that a LEADer leading self is a vital key because when you are LEADing others, you are not only sowing information but small strands of the LEADer are also being imparted. Because there is a lack of this kind of information, we have people who are only amazingly good at what they do and bad at who they are. Character assassination riddles their legacies to the point that what good they once did is hardly remembered. And though it is true, no one will have a squeaky-clean reputation, we should have the best resumes of diligence, integrity, and character.

I remember when I was called to preach. My grandfather, who is my hero, was the first person I told. I remember that day like yesterday. I was trimming his hair in the kitchen when I told him that I was going to be a preacher.

He turned and looked at me with tears welling up in his eyes and the warmest smile on his face. It was as if he already knew. Then he gave me one single piece of advice. He said, *"Son, don't be a lying preacher because your word is all you've got."* He didn't give me any other advice than that. There wasn't any advice on what to do - no advice on how to preach. My hero gave me advice on who I needed to be. It was advice on character and integrity. I have had many people give me advice throughout the years, but that one piece of advice still sticks with me. As I matured, I realized that the advice my grandfather gave me was not only one of character but also God's advice. I discovered that the only thing God has is His Word. He cannot lie (Numbers 23:19), His Word cannot return void (Isaiah 55:11), He can't break His Word (Hebrews 6:18), He stands by what He says (Psalms 138:2), and His Word is a settled matter (Psalms 119:89). It is clear that God was serious about what He said. Because of His Word, we can trust in Him to lead us. So, my grandfather's advice aligned me with the One I told him I would speak on behalf of. God's character can be trusted because His Word can be trusted. I learned quickly that if I was going to be a good LEADer, I couldn't just have the skillset; there should be found in me the foundation of what it means to LEAD.

We don't just need LEADers who can teach us what to do. We need LEADers who are doers themselves in what they teach. LEADers must be very careful not to fall into the trap of presenting a flawless package while disregarding their personal obligation to be the best versions of themselves. The apostle Paul pointed out that from his life you could not only follow his teachings but also his lead, *that ye be not slothful, but followers of them who through faith and patience inherit the promises* (Hebrews 6:12). He was clear and proficient in his assignment to the people but also consciously aware and accountable of the personal discipline he needed for himself, *but I keep under my body, and bring it into subjection: lest that by any means, when I have preached to others, I myself should be a castaway* (I Corinthians 9:27).

We don't just need LEADers. We need morally effective LEADers like never before. Even more, we need LEADers who have the character to match. When things are in upheaval, people look to strong, capable LEADers who can step up, be trusted, and are worth following. **We shouldn't have LEADers with good words who have to ignore and make excuses for their actions.**

True LEADership does not start with what you know. Let me preface this by saying it is vitally important that a LEADer possesses the wisdom and skill to gather the people and move them as one. But **true LEADship starts with who you are. This means that it also matters what the person is LEADing out of.** This then deals with the heart of the LEADer. "*A man is better kept by character and integrity than by gift, strategy, and talent alone.*" People are not only receiving from the person who is LEADing their skill set, but some of that person is being imparted to them. King Saul had all the capabilities of what a LEADer needed to be; the Bible says that he was head and shoulders to all men, but pride and arrogance caused him to lose the throne. And in addition, the people of God were brought under the yoke of their enemy.

In this book, we will be discussing Kingdom LEADership. Kingdom LEADership far exceeds the requirements of the world. In the world, leading is only performance-based. It does not demand or require the leader to be a person of character. Just that they have the ability to do the job and do it well. This is not the type of LEADer we will be discussing. I have realised that **there is too much focus on the skillset and not enough on the person who possess it**. We will side with a person based on party affiliation, history, and connection, knowing they are not suited for the job. We cannot afford to have people lead, knowing that their proclivities, shortcomings, and weaknesses far exceed their work capacity. What I've come to realise is that we overfocus on skill. God often uses the overlooked and underrated. But with the right heart and spirit, they overachieved. It is the part of us that goes ignored, unmastered, and unguarded that gets us. The trap of being so busy leading others that the need to be led gets lost in the sauce.

My aim is to keep it simple and straightforward. We all need partnering that will pull our coat tail - someone who can see our blind side and be that constructive warning for our greater good. **No height or growth of any LEADer makes them void of the reinforcement of accountability**.

My prayer is that this book will be that. I want the LEADer reading this book to realise that the vessel is just as important as the gifts, talents, and skills **working through it**. When the vessel is tainted, the gifts, talents, and skills eventually become tainted. Pride and arrogance don't come in the most recognisable forms, and even though you have mastered how to lead, you still have a part of you that you must be deliberate in being the LEADer of; *I discipline my body like an athlete, training it to do what it should. Otherwise, I fear that after preaching to others I myself might be disqualified* (I Corinthians 9:27NLT).

This book is about becoming a particular you, a LEADer. **What the world often gets away with becomes the great collapse of those leading in the Kingdom**. Success isn't only defined by how well you are at what you do but also by the character of the person you are. *The integrity and moral courage of the upright will guide them, But the crookedness of the treacherous will destroy them* (Proverbs 11:3 AMPC).

"God First, Others Second, Me Last. God is my Source."

When I became a full-time pastor, this became one of my main confessions as I prayed. The one thing I was never short of was confidence. Though I never asked for the front stage, I was never nervous when I got there. When I joined the church that birthed me into the LEADer and teacher I am today; I remember meeting Deacon Scott

Miller Sr. I was just drawn to him. He had the aura of God emanating from him. I was this new kid, but something in me wanted and knew that I needed - to connect. So, I walked up to Deacon Miller and asked how I could help the church, and he said, "Meet me here Sunday morning at 7 a.m." And that's where leading started for me. It started with me showing up early in the morning and just picking up the trash around the church. It was the greatest joy to see the church grounds looking immaculate. I'd follow him inside and do whatever needed to be done. I got to that church following my wife, who was then my girlfriend. Things started moving really fast for me in ministry. The pastor was very keen on starting on time. Someone better be up and starting service when it's time, or everyone was in trouble. He taught that we were lying to God when we say that church starts at a certain time on the sign and there is no activity at that time. He also believed that we could miss what Holy Spirit wanted to do, asking Him to meet us at 11 a.m., but we didn't get started until 11:01 a.m. That was okay with me because I was a former military, and timing was drilled into us. Fast-forward to this day, the church I now pastor has only started church late once, and it was when we shared the gym with the kids, and I would like to say Holy Spirit broke out, but actually, kid pandemonium broke, and we had to put the chairs back in order.

One particular Sunday, the pastor was attending to what I thought was an emergency. I saw the time was awfully close, so I went back to find the minister who usually led the corporate prayer, and he was in the office with the pastor, as were other men and Deacon Miller. I knocked on the door, and a minister peeked his head out. I pointed at my watch and said we have one minute till service starts. He closes the door in my face, then opens it back up and says, "The pastor says you do it." Do what! I've never done corporate prayer before, and there are many scriptures to quote. Corporate prayer is when the congregation repeats after you as you lead them in confessing the Word. I'm thinking that I'm new here, and these people aren't going to receive me. I had all these thoughts going through my mind while, at the same time, I was walking into the sanctuary to the stage. What in the world was I thinking? It's as if something is leading me straight up to the pulpit. I grab the mic and say, God, you are first, others second, and I'm last; you are my source. Please, God, don't let me bomb. I look up at the clock, and at zero minutes, I start my introduction, and I don't remember a thing that happened. I only remember the other men and the pastor coming out and smiling and saying good job; I knew you could do it. It turns out it was a setup. From then on, I did corporate prayer every morning.

> "The most meaningful part of leading is the soberness of remaining faithful to the One that has called you to lead."

A service I will never forget was a time we were having a conference and the house was packed. The room was electric. You could feel the spirit of God in the room. The people were responding with great expectation. It was powerful, and I got caught up. I got caught up in the people's response and took it as if it was for me. And in an instant, something happened. I could not remember one single scripture. It was the most frightening moment of my life. I literally felt dumb. I did not know what to say next. In my mind, it looked like the TV when it lost a signal. Even the people looked like they were moving in slow motion. I immediately knew what it was, and I started crying. I took glory and praise from God. It became me first. Mind you, all this is happening in my head, and it is happening in milliseconds. I started praying in the Spirit and repented to God immediately, and I heard the Spirit of the Lord say, "Don't you ever think that this is about you. I alone get all the glory and honour. Your job is to point My people to Me and not you!" And just as quickly as the scriptures left, they came back. And again, this all happened in milliseconds.

I will never forget that moment. I am glad that it happened and that it happened to me as a young minister. I believe that somewhere before we get to the ultimate stage of our call, we get to confront and challenge what could potentially ruin us on the big stage. Some see it and learn the lesson, while others ignore it. I didn't only learn the lesson, but I also promised God and myself that I would never flunk that test again. That moment has stuck with me ever since. And because of that, I never get on any stage and think it's about me. When people talk about how well I taught or spoke, I immediately say, "It's God; I'm just the vessel."

I take no credit, and I'm cautious about how much praise I receive. I always say, "Lord, don't let the people see me, but let my life point them to you." See, no amount of study or preparation can override the fact that it all comes from God, and in those moments, we are simply vessels being used by God. It started with a call - nothing you created, but one that was put upon you to represent someone else. Saul lost his position as king because he made one moment about him. From that one experience, I learned that it was important that I acknowledge that **God is first, others are second, and I am last because God is my source.**

Many would respond to this statement by saying that you need to ensure you are good first. Well, I'd like to push back and ask, "Who are you being good for?" Or better said, "Who is the one that is making you good?" Even when you study, it is to show yourself approved **unto God.** See, this is where LEADers are missing it. That slippery slope of delusion turns the LEADer from dependence and trust in God working through them to depending upon themselves. It then shifts from time in His presence and leaning on Holy Spirit to how much study time, quotes from others, and studies of others we have gleaned from. *Are you so foolish and so senseless and so silly? Having begun [your new life spiritually] with the [Holy] Spirit, are you now reaching perfection [by dependence] on the flesh?* (Galatians 3:3 AMPC). The Bible says that Jesus *made Himself of no reputation.* I believe that the awards and accolades that the world gets through performance have somehow convinced the

LEADers of the Church, Jesus' Bride, that they need some form of earthly validation like them.

The greatest validation you could ever receive is that God chose you to LEAD and chose you as His representative, flawed and all. He has obligated Himself to ensure that you are rewarded, so we don't have to take His: *Yours, O Lord, is the greatness, the power, the glory, the victory, and the majesty. Everything in the heavens and on earth is yours, O Lord, and this is your kingdom. We adore you as the one who is over all things* (II Chronicles 29:11 NLT). The greatest reward to a Kingdom LEADer is "**well done though a good and faithful servant,**" = reward "**though has been faithful** over a few things, **now I will make you** ruler over many." When it comes to LEADing - God **FIRST** - other **SECOND** - you **LAST, God is the source**.

The overall message in this book to the LEADer is that **you are LEADing, not just in what you say and do; you are LEADing in who you are**. All fruit comes from inside the tree. So, in the fruit lies what's in the tree. The reason we can depend on God's Word is because God is one with His Word, and you are also born again by the Word. You should not get a different version of the person giving. The teacher should be just as dependable as the lesson, *for the tree is known by his fruit* (Matthew 12:33c).

| Chapter 1

Heart to Please God

LEADer Note:
Do all things with God's heart and mind
on your heart and mind.

So above all, guard the affections of your heart, for they
affect all that you are. Pay attention to the welfare of
your innermost being, for from there flows the
wellspring of life -
Proverbs 4:23TPT.

King Solomon

Solomon started as an excellent LEADer. He was the
successor of his father, King David. He rehearsed before
God his great kindness towards his father as he walked
before God in truth, righteousness, and uprightness of
heart. Solomon admitted that he did not know how to go
out and come in before the people and asked God to give
him an understanding heart, to judge God's people, and
to discern between good and evil. And God gave Solomon
wisdom, understanding, and largeness of heart, even as
the sand on the seashore. Solomon's wisdom excelled the
wisdom of all the children of the East and all the wisdom

of Egypt. He was wiser than all men, and his fame was known in all nations. He also spoke three thousand proverbs and one thousand and five songs. Solomon had the wisdom of trees, from the cedar tree to the hyssop that came out of the wall. He also spoke of beasts, fowl, creeping things, and fishes. His wisdom had no categorical limit. All the people came to hear the wisdom of Solomon. Even all kings of the earth (I Kings 4).

Solomon did not start this way. He was a valiant, wise LEADer. His wisdom and prosperity were beyond fame. He only wanted wisdom and understanding from God to lead the people in the right direction. And while the wisdom and understanding given to him helped guide the affairs of others, kings, and their kingdoms, it did not cover Solomon's personal responsibility of guarding his heart. Though Solomon led with God's wisdom, he did not guard his own heart. And eventually, with an unguarded heart, he loved many strange women, and they turned his heart away from God. He went after a strange goddess, abominable idols, built high places (shrines) for them, and allowed his wives to burn incense and sacrifice unto their idol gods (I Kings 11). He was a very hard taskmaster who put a yoke upon the people (I Kings 12:7-11).

From Solomon's Lead

Gifts are not given to protect or work on the person they were given to. We must guard ourselves from what God gives us that makes us great. This can only come from a heart that is centered on pleasing God, not just success at doing the work. If the heart is not guarded properly, it will lead to personal failure. Never assume that because the gift and skill are producing results, the heart is good.

A LEADing Heart

There is a difference between having the heart to do something and having the heart to please God in what you do. The LEADer Note is one that I quote to myself as a reminder before I ever touch a pulpit or stage to speak. Before becoming a pastor, I was on the motivational speaker circuit and beginning to move up before God called me away to preach. My life goal was to be a travelling motivational speaker. Honestly, I actually love the behind-the-scenes. I love serving more than anything. Just the joy of seeing it all come together and helping others be their best was always a great motivation for me. Once I got moved from the back to the front, so to speak, I wanted to make sure that I kept that same heart and that my heart stayed in the right place. The front comes with a lot of admiration, attention, accolades, and applause, and if you are not careful, you can easily become removed from the very reason you were put there. It's not that applause isn't okay, but if the heart isn't in the right posture, you can pat yourself on the back, thinking it was you that got yourself to where you are.

Everything we are comes from the Creator above, and He alone should get the glory. So, I had to ensure that I guarded my heart from becoming contaminated by good works and achievements. The source of all man's doings comes from the heart. Whatever you are doing, it will eventually mimic your heart's posture. This is why we are warned by wisdom to pay attention to the welfare of our innermost being. The scripture says to guard it. Guards are put in place to protect something from being stolen or vandalized.

> When talents, gifts, and skills become the basis of one's trust, failure sits in the windshield of destiny.

I believe that LEADing with one's heart is the one area that, over time, becomes overlooked by the LEADer and thus causes many to fall. It is not that they do not start out with a heart of right intent, but intent must be fostered to maintain the heart's condition. Whereas it was once the place where every action flowed from, it now becomes a matter of being mind-information driven rather than committing to having the necessary information but leading from a God-centered heart. It must become something that is cultivated and held with the highest regard. The heart can be easily overlooked, given the equating value of what we are learning for the growth of our intellect. But Jeremiah 17:9 says that *"the heart is deceitful above all things, and desperately wicked: who can know it?"* However, verse 7 shares how to stay clear of the heart's ability to become a wicked vice, *"Blessed is the man that trusteth in the Lord, and whose hope the Lord is."* This word trust means *to have reliance upon, to look to.* The "eth" means on an ongoing, continual basis. So, even though you've got it and are prepared, you are still leaning your heart towards God in complete confidence and trust.

When wisdom and creativity flow through you and you've improved your skills, it can give off the impression of God's approval. But gifts and skills can work apart from a heart to please God because God is working through you for the greater good of others. The gifts and skills do not speak to the heart's condition. If so, the wisest man should have never turned from God but grew closer. No matter how well-tuned a motor or well-built an electric car is, they go nowhere without fuel or charge. God is our human fuel/charge.

> The most dangerous place for a LEADer is when he or she becomes talent- and gift-driven.

LEADers don't fail as a result of doing. LEADers fail because their heart no longer points towards the God that they are doing it for. I call this "heart hijacked." Satan wants you to be talent- and gift-driven because it's the easiest way to hijack a Believer's heart. It's a sifting process, though. This is one of his tactics that goes under the radar. The LEADer doesn't assume that they are moving from God because their gifts and abilities are working, and manifestation is even happening. The thought is that God must be involved, or else there would be a kink. On one side, God is involved. His Word cannot return void, and the gifts and callings are without repentance. On the other side, gifts, anointings, and talents have nothing to do with the position of the heart, *but we have this treasure in earthen vessels, that the excellency of the power may be of God, and not of us* (II Corinthians 4:7). **It's not weak LEADers that fall; it's great LEADers with weak hearts**. An additional deception that occurs is in the LEADer's mind is a push to do better, as if that is pleasing God and compensating for their heart condition. The LEADer now feels validated by their state because of what the work is producing, all the while falling deeper and deeper into the control of their carnal nature. Eventually, the heart becomes hijacked.

Having the Heart of God

This people draweth nigh unto me with their mouth, and
honoureth me with their lips;
but their heart is far from me.
Matthew 15:8

In order to have a heart for God, the LEADer needs to know what God's heart is. Having a heart of God does not just mean that you have a desire to please God. It also means that you have on your heart what's on God's heart, *But God removed Saul and replaced him with David, a man about whom God said, 'I have found David son of Jesse, **a man after My own heart**. He will do everything I want him to do* (Acts 13:22NLT). The first thing we see in this verse is that David was <u>after</u> God's heart. David did not earn this title because he was the cleanest man and always got it right. As a matter of fact, his life resume would seem to discredit him if such a statement ever was made about him, and based on this book's focus, he shouldn't be mentioned. David was chosen because he was in pursuit of the heart of God and stayed in pursuit. Secondly, God said that David would do everything I wanted him to do. Now, to do what God wants, you would first have to know what He wants, hence knowing what is on His heart.

To the Kingdom LEADer, it is not about their agenda; it is about God's agenda. The Kingdom LEADer has been bought with a price, and it is with their bodies that they should glorify God. Kingdom LEADers are officiants serving on behalf of God, and it's the King's agenda that they are sent to fulfil. *So we are Christ's ambassadors, God making His appeal as it were through us. We [as Christ's personal representatives] beg you for His sake to lay hold of the divine favour [now offered you] and be reconciled to God* (II Corinthians 5:20 AMPC).

A Servant's Heart

> But they held their peace: for by the way they had disputed among themselves, who should be the greatest. 35 And He sat down, and called the twelve, and saith unto them, If any man desire to be first, the same shall be last of all, and servant of all.
> Mark 9:34-35

Believe it or not, one of the easiest things to do in ministry is to dismiss God. From a positional standpoint, LEADers are often in the position of being looked to or looked up to. That is, they are often the ones that are being served - looked after. There is often a huge dependence on what they bring to the table. As a pastor, the Church and my team rely on me to forecast the vision and direction of the Church. So, the LEADer is being pulled mentally, emotionally, and spiritually first. But here is where it gets tricky. LEADers often become very engaged with how they have been engineered to solve problems and handle matters. With the exception of needing current and updated information, the operation procedure becomes second nature, almost to the point that it can **feel like** you are doing it yourself.

There are three things that LEADers need to be aware of. God gives every man three things: Spiritual gifts, natural talents, and acquired skills. Gifts work outside of the person's condition. Talents are a part of the biological and genetic makeup of man. And skills can be improved upon naturally. These are given by God to every man, and God does not take them back. Yet they are still connected to God. Meaning God has made a way in creation that He can work through creation, *every good gift, and every perfect gift is from above, and cometh down from the Father of lights, with who, is no variableness, neither shadow of turning* (James 1:17). Because they come from God and are still in connection to God, they have this somewhat autopilot capability. That capability can easily cause the LEADer to minister without God because they feel like God is with them because of what's working. And He is, but only in the gifts, talents, and skills.

The protection from this is a servant's heart. The LEADer must hold him or herself responsible for finding ways to maintain a servant's heart because they are usually the ones who are being served. *Who, being in the form of God, thought it not robbery to be equal with God: ⁷ but made Himself of no reputation, and took upon Him the form of a servant, and was made in the likeness of men ⁸ and being found in fashion as a man, **He humbled Himself**, and became obedient unto death, even the death of the cross. ⁹ **Wherefore God also hath highly exalted Him**, and given him a name which is above every name* (Philippians 2:6-9).

> The LEADer's heart is seen because it is the place that they lead from. You can have it in the head and never lead with your heart.

Jesus was the one LEADing the twelve, but Jesus was also the one who was a servant to the twelve, *Jesus knowing that the Father had given all things into His hands, and that He was come from God, and went to God; ⁴ He riseth from supper, and laid aside His garments; and took a towel, and girded Himself. ⁵ After that He poureth water into a bason, and began to wash the disciples' feet, and to wipe them with the towel wherewith He was girded* (John 13:3-5).

There are some vital keys that these two scriptures present that help explain why having a servant's heart is so important for a LEADer.

LEADer

V.3 - that the Father had given all things in His hands

LEADer Key:
God is in Heaven, and Jesus, as the Son of God, is on earth. So, in order that the Father be seen, He gives to His sons of God (Kingdom LEADers), His ability, so that through His ability working through them (sons), the people see the Father.

V.4 - He riseth from supper

LEADer Key:
The LEADer is proactive, intentional, and calculated. The fact that supper hadn't ended suggests that Jesus was out front and in the lead of how to serve.

V.4a - laid aside His garment

LEADer Key:
LEADers must be willing to take off their title.

V.4b - took a towel, and girded Himself

LEADer Key:
No LEADer is too great to serve; he should serve and know what is required of a servant. Also, servanthood is a garment. And note that it wasn't far from Jesus.

V.5 - poured water into a basin

LEADer Key:
The LEADer should be able to give back to others what others often give to the LEADer.

V.5a - began to wash the disciples' feet

LEADer Key:
Every LEADer should be found at some point serving those who serve them.

V.5b - and to wipe them with the towel wherewith He was girded...

LEADer Key:
The service should come from the LEADer, and not from them leading others to serve for them.

There will be followers, but it is the duty of LEADers to ensure that their examples of LEADership are building in others the spiritual character of a LEADer and not just skill. I believe that the greatest of LEADers are those who were once servants of others. The moral and character development, the wisdom poured in, and the lessons learned simply from an observatory perspective. Those small moments of wisdom being poured out and taught by the untaught but seen are incomparable to any form of teaching. This is what I learned from O.J.T (on-the-job training) and not from a class or conference. And so, **the LEADer must be mindful of the LEADership demonstrated through serving**. Looking back, I followed my pastor to meetings and sat in the corner while he talked through scriptures with others; all this was building in me the foundation of a LEADer.

Protecting the Heart

> Create in me a clean heart, O God;
> and renew a right spirit within me –
> Psalms 51:10.

A heart to please God is a posture. The posture of one's heart drives the intent and motives of the "why" and the "what" and is also the conductor of your manners. When Daniel was promoted over presidents and princes, the Bible says that they sought to find a way to bring accusations against Daniel concerning the kingdom and how he operated. It says they could find no occasion or fault, for Daniel was faithful, nor was there any error or fault in him (Daniel 6:1-4). Daniel had the heart to please God. When we are first introduced to him in Chapter 1, the first thing that is spoken of is Daniels's heart. It says, *But Daniel purposed* <u>*in his heart,*</u> *that he would not defile himself with the portion of the king's meat, nor with the wine which he drank* (Daniel 1:8). Because of their hearts, Daniel and the three Hebrew boys looked healthier. God gave them knowledge and skill in all learning and wisdom. Daniel had understanding in all visions and dreams, and they were ten times better than all the magicians and astrologers in the whole realm. The key thing here is that <u>because of the hearts</u> **God gave them**. They didn't work for it; it was a supernatural impartation that they not only received but continued throughout their lives. I am not saying that our hearts determine whether or not we receives gifts. Every good and perfect gift comes from above and God gives at His discretion. But I am most definitely saying that the proficiency of the

Heart to Please God

gift, and the level at which LEADers are used of God, are directly connected to the spirtual temperment of the heart.

It is critical that LEADers get the right heart from the start. Most LEADers use prayer and quiet time to ruminate and reflect on their vision and assignments. But even more so, prayer and quiet time must become a time of self-reflection. It is a time of looking over the conduits of one's heart to see if its posture has changed and if there is any diversion from its original intent. **You cannot be so driven by goal-achieving that heart posture is not also part of the goal**. And not just the goal, but the win. People have a change of heart all the time. What I've come to discover is that it wasn't that their heart changed; the heart was not being nurtured. And what was once a LEADing emanating from a cultivated heart is now coming from a heart that has become calloused. It can be so easily overlooked. **When driven to become a good steward and better at what you do, self-absorption can delude the relativeness of inner balance.** Little by little, the heart is turning from its origin. It is the sifting mechanism. The slight pivots of rotation aren't felt or seen. And this isn't deliberate, but it's the unintended casualties that do the most harm, *not with eyeservice, as menpleasers; but as the servants of Christ, **doing the will of God from the heart*** (Ephesians 6:6). The heart to please God will always keep the LEADer steady on course, *Trust in the Lord with all thine heart; and lean not unto thine own understanding. In all*

33

thy ways acknowledge him, and he shall direct thy paths (Proverbs 3:5-6).

Lastly, we must protect the heart from what I call "people persuasion." Everybody wants to know that they are doing or have done a good job. And feedback does provide some form of validation. However, too much of that could easily shift one's focus from ensuring that people are pleased to whether God is pleased. This is why a heart to please God is so important to a Kingdom LEADer. There is a place in the heart of a Kingdom LEADer that has to have far more connection to God than to people. I almost want to say that it has to have all kinds of connections to God in this area. The reason I say this is because, quite often, you will have to lead people by being the only one who understands and knows where you are going. And if you rely on the people's feedback rather than knowing you've heard God, then you are not God-led; you are people-driven. The job of a LEADer is not to give the people what they want but to give them what they need. **This requires that a LEADer be God-led and not emotionally driven**. Point your passion and emotions back to having a heart for God, which in turn will keep you having a heart for leading people the right way. *Moreover as for me, God forbid that I should sin against the Lord in ceasing to pray for you: but I will teach you the good and the right way* (I Samuel 12:23).

| Chapter 2

A Relationship with Christ

*The Lord is my Rock, my Fortress, and my Deliverer; my
God, my keen and firm Strength in Whom I will trust and
take refuge, my Shield, and the Horn
of my salvation, my High Tower.*
Psalms 18:2 AMPC

Apostle Paul

You would think that one would have selected one of the apostles who walked with Jesus to use as a character witness as an example of what it means to have a relationship with Christ. But I saw Paul as a more befitting person to use, simply because you and I will not see Jesus in this dispensation. We have been given Holy Spirit, who is Christ in us. It would be easy to see how one might have a relationship since they actually walked with the Saviour. But Paul is best because it was a life interruption and revelation that brought Paul into this amazing relationship with Christ, to the degree that he writes over three-quarters of the New Testament. Why wasn't it by one of the ones who walked, slept, and ate with Christ? Shouldn't the physical engagement of the other apostles point to greater understanding and a closer relationship? Not so. And this is why Paul is best suited. In Galatians, Paul reveals to us what actually deepens one relationship and what deepened his with Christ, *For I neither received it of man, neither was I taught it, but by the revelation of Jesus Christ* (Galatians 1:1). Paul knew Christ, without having walked with Him, because to have walked with someone does not mean that you know them. Christ is as close to you as anything could be because He is in you as Holy Spirit. You have the ability to have a relationship with Him in a way that the people of old died in faith to attain (Hebrews 11:13). For the New Testament Church, the promise of the Father lies within us.

From Paul's Lead

Paul reveals to us the depth of the relationship we can have with Christ; even though we do not physically walk with him, we can have the same experiential walk with Him because He lives in us. Paul was not short of impartation, revelation, or dedication; in fact, he may have had a deeper relationship with Christ than all of the other apostles. Jesus is the Word, so daily time in prayer and with your Bible would give you just as much of an up-close relationship as those who walked with him.

A Relationship with Christ

What is missing from most Kingdom LEADers today is a Christ revelation, relationship, and partnership with LEADing. Most of our teaching has made the relationship with God personal and just the sharing of Christ the public duty. The only focus on Jesus is His death, burial, resurrection, and return. Yet the Bible has so much more to say about Christ. I submit to you that Kingdom LEADing is LEADing out of Christ and not just talking about or referencing Him. You should have fruit that speaks of Christ reigning in your life. Across the board, many LEADers claim Christ, but their LEADing does not bear that relationship. There is a difference when someone is LEADing in Christ from the heart than from their head claiming Christ. Jesus attributes His LEADing as the work of the Father. And if His work was of the Father then our work should be of the Son, *Believe Me, that I am in the Father, and the Father in Me: or else believe Me for the very works' sake* (John 14:11). What this reveals is that from your lead, your relationship with Christ should be seen. We can't LEAD from a name-drop. We should LEAD out from the relationship that we have with Christ.

- ♦ We grow up into Him in all things (Ephesians 4:15).
- ♦ We are the body, and He is the head (Ephesians 1:22-23).
- ♦ We ask in His Name, and He is the Way, the Truth, and the Light. You don't get to the Father except through Him (John 14:6,16:23-24).
- ♦ We have power over the enemy through His Name (Luke 10:17).

- Holy Spirit is Christ in us (John 14:17-18, Colossians 1:27).
- Everything bows in the Name of Christ (Philippians 2:10).
- We are saved by Christ Jesus (Acts 4:12, Romans 10:9-13
- We reign as kings through the One-man Jesus (Romans 5:17 AMPC).
- It is His Kingdom that we live in (Colossians 1:13)
- We have redemption through His blood - the forgiveness of sin (Colossians 1:14).
- He is the image of the invisible God (Colossians 1:15).
- He saves us from our sins (Matthew 1:21).
- He created all things (Colossians 1:16).
- In Him all fullness dwells (Colossians 1:19).
- He is Alpha and Omega (Romans 1:8).
- Salvation is being given the Name of Jesus (Hebrews 2:10)
- Everything we do is in the Name of Jesus (Colossians 3:17).
- **Every book in the Bible points to Jesus.**

There is no relationship with God apart from Jesus. You will be amazed at the number of LEADers who are in a relationship with their talent, call, and gift but have no relationship with Christ. The deception is often, "I'm being my best for God." But how is being your best for God possible if the relationship is only with the objects that He has given to you that make you better suited for the use of Him? He still wants a relationship with the one to whom He entrusts those things. This is one of the exact reasons why God embodied flesh as Christ Jesus, to demonstrate firsthand to us how a relationship looks with Him. And while in that body as Christ Jesus, He even announced that body's dependence on God working through Him to get the work done, *I can of Mine own self do nothing: as I hear, I judge: and My judgment is just; because I seek not Mine own will, but the will of the Father which hath sent Me* (John 14:30). Remember this statement:

> "Different types of seeds produce
> different types of harvest."

Your life will ultimately manifest what you are in a relationship with. When a LEADer begins to sound like they are away from Christ, chances are that they are. Those tell-tell signs always show up. It is fatalistic to assume that because the gift is working, the skill is improving, the talent is recognised, and people's lives are changing, that means your relationship with Jesus is rock solid. **Being excellent in your talent, skill, and gift does not equate to having a relationship with Jesus**. *Many will say to me in that day, Lord, Lord, have we not prophesied in thy Name? and in thy Name have cast out devils? And in thy Name done many wonderful works? 23 And then will I profess unto them, I never knew you: depart from Me, ye that work iniquity* (Matthew 7:22-23). In this very text, Jesus is saying that things can be done in His Name by a person, and that person is not known of Him. In Acts 19:15-16, some exorcists attempted to cast an evil spirit out in the Name of the Lord Jesus, *And the evil spirit answered and said, Jesus, I know, and Paul, I know;* **but who are ye?** *16 And the man in whom the evil spirit was leaped on them, and overcame them, and prevailed against them, so that they fled out of that house naked and* *wounded.* The point again is someone attempting to work in the Name with whom they had no relationship.

The development of your relationship with Christ Jesus surmounts anything that you do because everything in your life becomes built, balanced, and sustained by and through that relationship. It is the one relationship that exceeds all else. My warning to LEADers is to strive to be the best in everything that you do. We need effective LEADers like never before. But the key to your effectiveness is not how great you are but how great of a relationship you have with Christ. The Pharisees and Sadducees were the smartest of their times, but When Jesus stepped on the scene teaching from the very same scroll that they had down to memory by heart, they were astonished at His doctrine, for He taught them as one that had authority, and not as the scribes. They called it a new doctrine. *For with authority, He commanded even the unclean spirits, and they obeyed Him* (Mark 1:21-28). This wasn't just because He was Jesus. **Jesus worked out His relationship with God, as LEADers should work out their relationship with Christ.** *The Son can do nothing of Himself, but what He seeth the Father do: for what things soever He doeth, these also doeth the Son likewise* - John 5:19. He also said that it was the Father at work in Him doing the work and His works bare witness of the Father. This relationship is important because there is the potential to point the people to the wrong source - the LEADer. When Kingdom LEADing is about pointing people back to the Lord of all, that being Christ.

Jesus spoke about the importance of a relationship with Him. He said that without the eating of His flesh and the drinking of His blood, the person had no life in them. And to those that did, they dwelled in Him, and He in them. This passage talks of the communion meal, which they should have completely understood. How could they know the law and think that Jesus was speaking of literal blood and bodily flesh? But you can see the difference here of having a relationship with customs, traditions, and doings absent from who they did it for. The Bible says that day many turned away from following Christ (John 6:52-66). Jesus then turns to Peter and asks if they would leave also and hear their reply; *then Simon Peter answered Him, Lord, to whom shall we go? <u>Thou hast the words of eternal life.</u>* **⁶⁹ And we believe and are sure that thou art that Christ, the Son of the living God** - John 6:68-69. You will not know Jesus as Christ, the Son of the living God, without a relationship. Peter said they <u>believed and were sure</u> about who He was.

Here lies the importance of a LEADer's relationship with Christ. As a Kingdom LEADer, there is an assurance that you must have about the One you are LEADing on behalf of. **Kingdom LEADers are accountable to the one they are the spokesperson for**. How can you LEAD or speak effectively on behalf of Christ if your relationship is only gift, talent, or skill-based, *And my speech and my preaching was not with enticing words of man's wisdom, but in demonstration of the Spirit and of power* - I Corinthians 2:4?

Christ Revealed Through You

I am crucified with Christ: nevertheless I live; yet not I, **but Christ liveth in me**: and the life which I now live in the flesh I live by the faith of the Son of God, who loved me, and gave Himself for me.

Galatians 2:2

It is LEADing through Christ that LEADers have to stay committed to. Everything should platform off that. Most advancement is measured through how effectively one can communicate or their status. But we are cautioned in the concerning only LEADing this way. LEADers should strive to have the best communication skill, and status is a promise, but promotion solely based on the flesh reaps corruption because it is a building on self and not on Him, *Though I might also have confidence in the flesh. If any other man thinketh that he hath whereof he might trust in the flesh, I more: 7 But what things were gain to me, those I counted loss for Christ. 8 Yea doubtless, and I count all things but loss for the excellency of the knowledge of Christ Jesus my Lord: for whom I have suffered the loss of all things, and do count them but dung, that I may win Christ* (Philippians 3:4,7-8).

Christ has to be more than a name. We see Christ in many instances from the Word, showing us that we can LEAD through Him in any environment. He is not limited to spiritual matters only. He does not want to be left out; He is the connecting piece. When you LEAD without Christ, you are limited to your skill, talent, and your strength. It is by His spirit, His might, and His power and not our own (Zechariah 4:6).

The relationship equation for the Believer is:

From God > To Us > Through Us > To Others

The LEADer doesn't pause on their relationship or who they have become in Christ in dealing with others. They LEAD through their relationship as Christ LEADs through them so that the people we come into contact with experience Christ in us as the shining light. *When the Council saw the boldness of Peter and John and could see that they were obviously uneducated non-professionals, they were amazed and realized what being with Jesus had done for them* (Acts 4:13 TLB).

No one should leave having spent time with us, being led by us, having worked with us, and not have experienced Him, or have an undeniable impression left with them, *My old self has been crucified with Christ. It is no longer I who live, but Christ lives in me. So, I live in this earthly body by trusting in the Son of God, who loved me and gave Himself for me* (Galatians 2:20 NLT). No one was the same after having shared proximity with Jesus. Be it the light that shineth in darkness exposing duplicity amongst the religious crowd sparking anger or question (Mark 1:22-28), or the abundant life being brought to the lost, no one was the same (Acts 10:38).

This should be the same outcome that others have as a result of encountering one of God's LEADers. *And they went forth, and preached every where, the Lord working with them, and confirming the Word with signs following. Amen* (Mark 16:20). **We aren't just LEADers; we are**

Kingdom change agents. The relationship that we have with Christ is not just one of inward growth, but one that should touch the lives of those with whom we have contact with. As we deepen our relationship with Christ, we deepen the extent of our reach to others. It is *Christ in us, the hope of glory* (Colossians 1:27), but it is also Christ through us to reach those who are lost.

| Chapter 3

Consistent Prayer Life

LEADer Note:
As blood is to the body, so prayer is to
your spirit man.

> Praying always with all prayer and supplication in the
> Spirit, and watching thereunto with all perseverance and
> supplication for all saints.
> **Ephesians 6:18**

Jesus

Many would say that it was easy for Jesus to overcome
the enemy's attacks; He was God in the flesh. But what is
not understood is that while God was in that body as
Jesus, that body did not house the infinite sovereignty of
God, and Jesus was subject to the functions of a body. He
slept, ate, was tempted, experience grief, and even
questioned the Father on the Cross. The Bible even
declares that Jesus grew, *And Jesus increased in wisdom
and stature, and in favour with God and man* (Luke 2:50).
The key to Jesus' success is the exact same key to ours - a
body submitted and dependent on Holy Spirit. Because it

was Jesus does not mean that He did not have to walk in the Spirit, nor trust God, *Then answered Jesus and said unto them, Verily, verily, I say unto you, **The Son can do nothing of Himself**, but what He seeth the Father do: for what things soever He doeth, these also doeth the Son likewise* (John 5:19). This means that Jesus had the same spiritual responsibilities that you and I have. He too had to have a consistent prayer life. If you took a deeper dive of study into the prayer life of Jesus, you would discover that it was from prayer that Jesus dealt with life's affairs. Jesus spent much time in prayer so that He could spend little time handling problems and casting out devils. When He was found in the midst of a storm, he was not up praying all night. He was found in the hinder part of the ship, asleep on a pillow. This is a starch contrast to where Christians are found in the storms of life. Prayer was the vehicle of Jesus' ministry. He stayed in constant contact with the Father, so He was always in step with what was on the Father's agenda. And if there were a pivot in the journey of stopping by Samaria, He was equipped enough spiritually to know that it was God.

Jesus' prayer life also gave Him an amazing level of confidence and boldness. When He raises Lazarus from the dead, the Bible says that they took the stone away, and then Jesus looks up and says these words in John 11:41-42, *Father, I thank thee that **though hast heard Me**, And **I know that thou hearest Me always**: but because of the people which stand by I said it, that they may believe that thou hast sent Me.* Jesus exemplifies the confidence and boldness necessary as a LEADer when dealing with life-threatening events, as you will as a Kingdom LEADer, but that only comes through a consistent prayer life.

From Jesus' Lead

From Jesus' LEAD, we learn that prayer is an essential component to the success of a LEADer. Often as LEADers, we seek out those things that make us better for the people and never consider that our prayer life sets the greatest presidency of those things. **Is it possible that thousands of dollars are spent yearly for conferences and seminars to better us as LEADers, which we should do, but the thing that those things get their effectiveness from is often left out?** Jesus spoke a parable that *men ought always pray and not faint* (John 18:1). This reveals to us possibly why LEADers are fainting - they aren't praying.

Jesus is the pattern, and from the pattern, we see that His success as a LEADer was developed and came out of His prayer consistency.

Consistent Prayer Life

LEADers can be very centered, and they should. But sometimes, their centerdness can LEAD to their demise. They falter in that they stop depending on the prayer life that elevated them and become dependent upon the growth of the gift and expansion in their assignment as the things that empower them. It is this misapprehension that the more growth, people, and assignment expansion, the more as a LEADer you need to be on your game. The truth is, **the higher you _go up_, the more in you need to _go in_.** And by in, I'm saying into prayer and God time. One morning when I went into my closet to pray, I have a closet in my house that I go into and pray; I heard Holy Spirit say, "This is how you live." Shortly after, our Church began to grow, and I felt the need to go deeper in my studies so that I would have something to give the people. But immediately, I remembered what Holy Spirit said to me that morning.

This prayer life is important because **you can actually give attention to a good thing at the wrong time**. We have been given Holy Spirit, whose assignment is to LEAD and guide us into all truth. However, if we aren't engaging the Spirit and getting God's heart for the people or our assignment, we miss out on what God intended to do. This often leads to immature growth, delayed growth, or no growth at all.

The LEADer making it their sole responsibility to have all that's needed to LEAD is very dangerous. _Are you so foolish and so senseless and so silly? Having begun [your new life spiritually] with the [Holy] Spirit, are you now reaching perfection [by dependence] on the flesh_ (Galatians 3:3 AMPC)? **It is not self-dependence; it's interdependence**. LEADers are not the sole contributor and should not make the people their responsibility. This is a false premise of a LEADer's centerdness. **LEADers are accountable to God, and in being accountable to**

God, they uphold their responsibility to the people. This is why the LEADer should have a consistent prayer life. **It is the prayer life that keeps the LEADer connected spirit to Spirit.** Prayer is what makes the power available to the LEADer to do what they do, *...the earnest (heartfelt, continued) prayer of a righteous man makes tremendous power available [dynamic in its working]* (James 5:16b AMPC). Yes, it can be done with the operation of knowledge and skill. But only for a short time because it does not have any power backing it. This is exactly why many secular LEADers fizzle out. If LEADing is the true objective, LEADers must see the need to be spiritually empowered first, then better in operation. Prayer is where the LEADer gets their power.

> It's not only important that Kingdom LEADers be backed by the Word, but that they are also empowered by prayer.

There is a disconnect that Kingdom LEADers must avoid. It is the exchange of work for one's commitment to prayer. LEADers must understand the difference between spiritual work that's done for others and spiritual work that is done for themselves, *but I keep under my body, and bring it into subjection: lest that by any means, when I have preached to others, I myself should be a castaway* (I Corinthians 9:27). It is easy to believe that time spent in preparation, teaching, and LEADing means that you have spent time with God. But there is no supplement for prayer. There is no substitute for your personal time with God for you.

The burnout, inner questioning, spiritual tiredness, and depression occurring amongst many LEADers often come from what I call *demonic delusional substitutes*. It's this thought that you are in the Word and around spiritual things all the time, so surely that accounts for time with God. The preparation for what you are doing for others is being imparted into you also. If this were the case, we would not have many LEADers falling into perverse acts. The operation of the gift can be very deceptive. I constantly have to remind myself and my team to be careful not to fall into the trap of assuming that because you work for the Church, at the Church, and much of your work is to the people of God on behalf of God, not to assume that it compensates for personal time with God or makes up for your personal spiritual nourishment. It is the most subtle trap.

> Do not make the mistake of dropping off your spiritual regimen, to pick it up later. It goes before you.

Kingdom LEADers are not policing themselves in this area as they should. The greatest part of Jesus' earthly ministry was not miracles and healing but His prayer life. Jesus was constant in stealing away to get along with the Father. He was persistent in staying connected to the power source. In II Corinthians 2:4-5, Paul expressed the importance of why our consistent connection to God is so important, *And my speech and my preaching was not with enticing words of man's wisdom, but in demonstration of the Spirit and of power: 5 that your faith should not stand in the wisdom of men, but in the power of God.* There is a danger in being connected to the call more than you are connected to God, which is an undetected disconnection. This is also what I call the *standing fall.* **Everyone sees this great LEADer doing amazing things, but what they don't see is the inward fall that's happening because they aren't connected to the power source because they don't have a sincere, consistent prayer life**, *also, [Jesus] told them a parable to the effect that they ought always to pray and not to turn coward (faint, lose heart, and give up)* (Luke 18:1 AMPC). If you pray and you won't faint is true, then the converse is also true: <u>if you don't pray, you are going to faint, lose heart and give up</u>. **God did not give LEADers gifts and skills to fuel their spirits**. These are extensions of Himself for earth, in the life of His people for others. God is the source, and the LEADer connects to the source through prayer, *for in Him we live, and move, and have our being; as certain also of your own poets have said, for we are also His offspring (*Acts 17:28).

> The longest prayer a LEADer can pray is: "Lord show me, me!"

Just like the Kingdom LEADer grows themselves in the knowledge of their skill and gift, they must also see prayer as a part of their growth. **The higher up the LEADer goes in the operation of their gift and skill, the higher their prayer life should be.** The Bible tells us that we need the armour of God to handle the things that are in high places. Prayer is a part of that armour, *praying always with all prayer and supplication in the Spirit, and watching thereunto with all perseverance and supplication for all saints* (Ephesians 6:18). How then are LEADers out front without the proper armour on? This is a setup for failure. Satan would love nothing more than for it to be the LEADer - the ones in the front.

It is important that a LEADer be in prayer concerning those that they are LEADing. This isn't the place where prayer is usually missed. **It is missed in the commitment of the LEADer to pray for themselves**. I've come to learn that praying away from yourself is easy. Taking the time to pray for myself presented difficulty until I learned what I was looking for. Personal prayer time allows for personal examination that other prayers don't focus on. The better you become at what you do, the more knowledgeable you need to be about your frailties. Paul said in 2 Corinthians 13:5 NLT, *examine yourselves to see if your faith is genuine. Test yourselves. Surely you know that Jesus Christ is among you; if not, you have failed the test of genuine faith.* Paul spoke of the importance of judging or self-examining himself. He put himself under spiritual scrutiny. He used the spiritual principle of prayer as the watchman of his soul. He put no trust in himself, his call, or his gifts. He noted them to be all dung for Christ's sake, *Yea doubtless, and I count all things but loss for the excellency of the knowledge of Christ Jesus my Lord: for whom I have suffered the loss of all things, and do count them but dung, that I may win Christ* (Philippians 3:8). Paul saw excellence not in how well he did or in the validation that came from people; he counted excellence as the knowing of Christ, his Lord.

Personal Devotion

O God, thou art my God; early will I seek thee: my soul thirsteth for thee, my flesh longeth for thee in a dry and thirsty land, where no water is.

Psalms 63:1

Personal devotion is the empowerment place for the Kingdom LEADer. It is the place where our roots are strengthened. Let me pause here and say that everyone is a LEADer in some area. God has given every Believer a sphere of influence. And it is in that space that God intends you to LEAD. This Kingdom LEADing has very little to do with the title. It deals more with the Kingdom's agenda of restoration and reconciliation, which, to simplify, means we are restoring and repairing what has been damaged by sin and reclaiming back to God the lives of those who are lost because of sin.

Vehicles today either need recharging or fuel. At some point in the journey, the driver has to pull over to fill up or recharge. You can have a perfect car with all the working parts, but without fuel or charge, that perfect vehicle will go nowhere.

This is what personal devotion is to the life of the LEADer. The burnouts and LEADers becoming frazzled is often due to the neglect of getting refuelled/recharged. It caters to a point I have made throughout this book. We need Him to do the work and do it effectively. The vehicles of gift, talent, and skill without fuel or recharge to the person operating in them will inevitably leave the person parked by the side of the road. I constantly communicate to my Executive Team that **because you work in the Church, which puts you around Godly things and handling Godly things all the time, it does not mean that it is a substitute for your personal time with God**. And you must also separate the study that you do for your job from the one still needed for yourself. I cannot stress how important this devotional piece is.

> The LEADer maintains their
> heart posture from the presence

Jesus would always be found stealing away from the crowd and even the disciples to spend alone time with God. In every letter that Paul wrote, you'll find him mentioned somewhere about how the Church was always in his prayers and how earnestly he was interceding for them. It's not the biggest thing, but it does hold a lot of power. The one thing that Satan will always try to disrupt is the Word (Mark 4:15) and a person's devotional time. And He does because, in both of these, you are being fueled by God. So, the less fuel you have, the shorter the drive you can take. He understands that we have to be clear that you can't go where you aren't fueled or charged to go. It doesn't matter how good the things in the vehicle are. If the vehicle doesn't have what it needs, the thing can't go. He knows that even the most gifted and talented LEADer will eventually run out if he or she ignores fueling. And what they don't realize is that an attack from the enemy is a slow sift.

What is your gas/charge needle reading? Are you running on fumes? Maybe you have been running solely on your own abilities. Have you been ignoring your personal time with God? Do you only get it corporately on a Sunday or midweek service? Do you intentionally set aside time to spend time with God so that you maintain the right heart posture? So that you can strengthen your relationship with Christ? So that you can commune with Holy Spirit? So that you can pray? If you have to pause to think, I submit that your fuel light is on. And if it's been on for a while, you are in reserve, and once that is gone, you will be forced to pull over. The sad irony of this pulling over is that most LEADers never recover the same. They ignored all the signs that Holy Spirit was giving them to avoid it. The other unfortunate about LEADing this way of LEADing low is that like a car that stays low on fuel, eventually trash from the bottom of the tank is pulled into the fuel lines, corrutptig the motor.

Make your devotional time just as important as you build your mind with the knowledge and skillset you need to be a better LEADer. **Life for you, the LEADer, is lived inside out**.

| Chapter 4

In-tune w/ Holy Spirit

LEADer Note:
The greatest relationship to a LEADer is Holy Spirit.

But the Comforter (Counselor, Helper, Intercessor, Advocate, Strengthener, Standby), the Holy Spirit, Whom the Father will send in My name [in My place, to represent Me and act on My behalf], He will teach you all things. And He will cause you to recall (will remind you of, bring to your remembrance) everything I have told you.
John 14:26 AMPC

One of the greatest partners given to a LEADer is Holy Spirit. It's having an advantage in life. Holy Spirit is definitely the difference maker. He makes you look extremely smart. Just as I was writing this book, we bought a set of cameras, and one of the cameras had an attachment that was not working properly. The LEADer over production looked through the manual, called, and even googled but could not find the problem. I prayed, and immediately Holy Spirit brought back to my memory a small portion of a clip that I saw in a video that was the way to fix the issue. The next day I went into the sanctuary with the production LEADer. I walked up to the camera lens and did what I saw in the video, and the attachment worked just as it should. The production LEADer asked me how I found out. I replied that Holy Spirit showed me. He knows everything. He just stared in amazement.

> Intellect is not a replacement for Holy Spirit.

This is what Holy Spirit does. You will be amazed at the number of things Holy Spirit reveals when you simply take the time to acknowledge Him and ask. He knows all things. As Kingdom LEADers, we have to be very careful of sole reliance on ourselves. *The "study to show yourself approved"* scripture can be over-read to think that our studies alone are what make us who we are. Only to some degree. Had it only been a matter of studying, Jesus would not have said that it was expedient for Him to go and to send Holy Spirit in His place. Pause there - if Jesus functioned on the earth by dependence on Holy Spirit, then why are LEADers functioning on the earth without dependence on Him? *For as many as are led by the Spirit of God, they are the sons of God* (Romans 8:14). True Kingdom LEADers are led by the Spirit of God. What this tells us is that not all that we will learn or is revealed will come from books. *But as it is written, eye hath not seen, nor ear heard, neither have entered into the heart of man, the things which God hath prepared for them that love Him. 10 But God hath revealed them unto us by His Spirit:*

for the spirit searcheth all things, yea, the deep things of God (II Corinthians 2:9-10).

I am always amazed at how many Kingdom LEADers make light of Holy Spirit. I believe this is because of what Westernized Christianity has purported in the Bible. Receiving Holy Spirit has been made the end-all, rather understanding that He is the beginning, *But ye shall receive power, after that the Holy Ghost is come upon you: **and ye shall be** witnesses unto Me both in Jerusalem, and in all Judæa, and in Samaria, and unto the uttermost part of the earth* (Acts 1:8).

The Bible is more than a sacred book. It is a life book that guides our daily lives, business, home, career, finances, etc. It's not just for the things that we deem as spiritual. It's a life book that Holy Spirit is the author of. To LEAD without being in tune with Holy Spirit is to LEAD without the One who authored life, and without the One for which you are leading, *He shall glorify Me: for He shall receive of Mine, and shall shew it unto you* (John 16:14). How then are you a Kingdom LEADer, whose main objective is to point people to Christ. To ensure the proper pointing, Jesus gives you Holy Spirit, who comes in His stead, so that you can point properly and you have no fellowship with Holy Spirit as a LEADer? The question now becomes, what are you LEADing with? And if the answer is your own intellect and study, then you are building people with a reliance upon you, when a Kingdom

LEADer's job is to build LEADers with a dependence on God.

> It must be Holy Spirit and not the LEADer's human spirit.

The greatest relationship to a Kingdom LEADer is with Holy Spirit. This point cannot be driven home enough. The one thing David did not want to be found out of relationship with was Holy Spirit, *... and take not thy Holy Spirit from me* (Psalms 51:11b). The Apostles, who had been given the call, commission, and command to go into the world, did no ministry until they were filled with Holy Spirit. They were told to tarry {wait} until they were endued with power from on High (Acts 2:4-8). Their LEADing needed the empowerment and backing of Holy Spirit. Kingdom LEADers need to function and operate in a power that is from on High. **Problems cannot be solved on the same level as the problem itself.** Kingdom LEADers are called to LEAD from a higher plain of wisdom and understanding. *This wisdom descendeth not from above, but is earthly, sensual, devilish. [17] But the wisdom that is from above is first pure, then peaceable, gentle, and easy to be intreated, full of mercy and good fruits, without partiality, and without hypocrisy* (James 5:15,17). The mind is limited in its retention ability. But with Holy Spirit, LEADers have a way to connect to the untapped and unlimited well of wisdom, knowledge, and understanding. Kingdom LEADers have no right to LEAD without being led by Holy Spirit. It is a carnal way of functioning spiritually, and it has dying consequences for the LEADer and those with whom they are leading. What the LEADer must understand is that they have not been given a freefall way of leading. Kingdom LEADers lead effectively when they are led, and that leading is from Holy Spirit, *for as many as are **led by the Spirit of God**, they are the sons of God* (Romans 8:14). Holy Spirit is the agent of God who LEADs us. Many times, LEADers pray and move. But this is an incorrect way of operation. We cannot pray past instruction, and Holy Spirit is in our lives to LEAD and guide us into all truth.

There does not have to be as many mistakes that are made in the Kingdom of God. The issue is that Holy Spirit is often not allowed to do the job He has been given. There are attributes that come with our being in tune with Holy Spirit that will always have us in the right place at the right time and doing things the right way. But that type of relationship has to be built. Looking back over every misstep, I can also see where God was sending words or warning about what to do or not to do. God gave us His Word and Holy Spirit as the teacher for our lives, not mistakes and missteps. *All scripture is given by inspiration of God, and is **profitable for doctrine, for reproof, for correction, for instruction in righteousness**: 17 that the man of God may be perfect, throughly furnished unto all good works* (II Timothy 3:16). And John 16:13a says, *Howbeit when He, the Spirit of truth, is come, **He will guide you** into all truth.*

Skill only does not allow LEADers to ascertain the spirit of the matter. Many missteps of LEADers happen because their thoughts, motives, and decisions are not run through Holy Spirit first. It's usually afterwards that LEADers turn to Him to correct the mistake rather than engaging Him from the onset so that the action aligns with God's will of success; r*oll your works upon the Lord [commit and trust them wholly to Him; He will cause your thoughts to become agreeable to His will, and] so shall your plans be established and succeed* (Proverbs 16:3 AMPC). **Kingdom LEADers have an edge**. This means they have an advantage. Believers have with them, in them, and One who wants to work through them - Holy Spirit. He has the solution to every problem, and the answer to every question. He can discern the need of everyone in the room and, through the speaking of one, give an answer to all. Holy Spirit not only sees further down the road but around the corner too. Holy Spirit who can bring everything back to remembrance and show you things to come. Why wouldn't a LEADer want a person with these capabilities on their side? Kingdom LEADers do! But it is their choice to make use of Him as such.

The Safeguard

> All things are lawful [that is, morally legitimate, permissible], but not all things are beneficial or advantageous. All things are lawful, but not all things are constructive [to character] and edifying [to spiritual life].
> I Corinthians 10:23 AMPC

Another great benefit of being in tune with Holy Spirit is His ability to aid you with your boundaries. Your body is the temple of Holy Spirit, and you have been bought with a price. Your central aim is to glorify God in your body. God knows what's best for your body. The things that are best suited and advantageous to your growth and character, and the things that will not cause your good to be evil, are spoken of. We should trust the whole of ourselves to these decisions, *For we are the circumcision, which worship God in the spirit, and rejoice in Christ Jesus,* **and have no confidence in the flesh** (Philippians 3:3). There will be lawful things that are off limits for you but totally permissible for someone else. Once Holy Spirit tags something as off limits to you, although it is not sinful, it has become a sin to you because you cannot walk out of faith in doing it. It is here that you will have to simply trust in the LEADing of Holy Spirit. He sees and knows what you don't see. Holy Spirit sees down the road and around the corner. So, what we cannot see happening or manifesting as a result of something seemingly lawful and unharmful can potentially be the thing that destroys the LEADer down the road.

> In all things be God led and not emotionally driven.

This is called suffering, for Chris's sake. Every LEADer has something that their purpose will cause them to have to suffer for Christ's sake. Sadly, many Kingdom LEADers never seek or hear Holy Spirit when He tags the thing. And because it is not sinful, they think it has no negative outcome in their lives. But these don't always have outcomes for us. Remember, as a LEADer, you are out front representing God. He is shining a light on you as His representative, and there are things that He has left off the plate concerning you. Will you suffer for Christ's sake? Is having or doing it that important?

My wife and I sacrifice tremendously. I knew at the onset what position I'd hold in the lives of people as God's man. And I did not want anything to hinder anyone's growth in God. It's an unfortunate thing, but people look to their LEADers differently than they do other people. Even the Bible says that if *you smite the shepherd, the sheep will scatter* (Mark 14:27). When I read this verse, it put a heavy conviction and respect for the LEADing position that God put me in. It was important that I point the people in the right direction and that my life represented that same pointing. **If you can't handle suffering for Christ as a LEADer in the innocence of things, hang that LEADer coat up today.** There is no room for selfish ambition as a LEADer. **You live for more than yourself when you say yes to being a LEADer.**

You don't know what things you may have to suffer in for the level of LEADship you have been called to. God may call you to a consistent life of fasting. It may be a place you can't go, a thing you can't do, food, or an activity that you can't partake in. It could be something that He doesn't want you to wear or ever say. For instance, one of the things God told me was never to count the people. Now on the business side, I get reports of visitors, attendance, and salvation, but I never count the people to determine if I can do what God says. My wife and I never post pictures of our bodies without clothing. There are some other things that Holy Spirit has put restrictions on about us, and I came to grips with them. I am amazed at how LEADers today ignore accountability. The scripture talks about our liberty becoming a stumbling block to the weaker brother, and how when we sin so against the brethren, and wound their weak conscience, we actually sin against Christ (II Corinthians 8:9,12). It's God's body. It's His life, not ours, and if it does not bring glory and honor to Him, LEADers shouldn't do it. Seek Holy Spirit for what things He wants you to avoid contact with, then settle on a *do not* with those things.

Unctioned by the Spirit

Next, they traveled through Phrygia and Galatia because the Holy Spirit had told them not to go into the Turkish province of Asia Minor at that time. 7 Then going along the borders of Mysia they headed north for the province of Bithynia, but again the Spirit of Jesus said no.
Acts 16:6-7

I'm using the word unction to mean *to have a sudden change of direction or doing that was not planned.* This is important because, to the best of the LEADer's study, planning, and preparation, there are still some unknowns. God may want to go in a different direction and even have something different to say compared to what you prepared for. The scripture says that we *study to show ourselves approved unto God* (II Timothy 2:15), not that God will use everything we study. Is the LEADer in tune enough to hear and willing to yield to the redirecting of Holy Spirit? Can God have His way? Does this mean that God disregards planning and cannot, in the planning, give in advance those directions? Of course not. In Acts 8, Phillip was told to arise and go south, where there was a man, a eunuch of great authority, under Candace, queen of the Ethiopians. It wasn't planned; Phillip didn't know in advance. But that moment of obedience got a man saved and baptised, and the Gospel of the Kingdom sent to Ethiopia (Acts 8:26-40).

It is never without trust and reliance upon the Spirit that Kingdom LEADers do anything. There are circles of ministry that adhere to that if God was going to do something special, He would use the planning moment to prepare the LEADer for it. This is dangerous and could be the furthest from the truth, which is why this conversation is important. Does God tell every prophet what they will prophesy before they prophesy? Does God give the Word of Wisdom or Knowledge before it is needed? Does He tell everyone what they are going to give in service before its time to give? I've paid for countless people's lunch and dinner and did not know that Holy Spirit would unction me to do so. Pause - what's an unction? I've stopped people and prayed for their loved ones I didn't know of, but Holy Spirit unctioned me to pray with them, and the prayer was spot on. I've had to change my entire message right before going up to preach. I have prepared to teach, and Holy Spirit takes over the service and says just worship Me. *The natural man receiveth not the things of the Spirit of God for they are foolishness unto him, neither can he know them*

66

because they are spiritually discerned (I Corinthians 4:15). It is okay if God does not give it all to you. This is where the trust and reliance upon Him come into play. The children of Israel were saved from being captured because the Spirit of God unction Elijah in telling them to go another way. Can you imagine the number of Believers who have died prematurely, missed opportunities, or fallen to the sword, all because they were not in tune with the functioning of the Spirit and stayed with the norm of their schedule?

> LEADers are in danger when leading with their head outside of their heart.

So many LEADers are relying solely on their own intellect. Many of our church services are so planned out that the One with whom the planning is for has no space to do different or go another way if He desires. Does the LEADer have the revelation to not only get in prayer for themselves but for the people that are coming? It could be at that prayer that they see the different direction they need to take that differs from the one they planned. We ask for Holy Spirit to LEAD and guide us, and when He does, His LEADing is unaccepted. Our church service motto is *We plan for an excellent service and respect the time, but Holy Spirit has the right to interrupt at will.* The disciples did no ministry work without Holy Spirit in them. And Jesus did no ministry work without Holy Spirit through Him, yet Kingdom LEADers are working their fields without knowing what an unction from Holy Spirit is like.

I recall one time I had to go to court. While putting on my clothes, I heard Holy Spirit say to wear a blue suit and white shirt. I get to court, and the judge is not in a good mood that day. Every person that walks up is getting the hammer. People are literally trying to walk out of the court and reschedule. It was not good. She wouldn't even allow some to speak. Then she called my name. I walked up, and she looked over her glasses and said case dismissed. What? It was a shock to me and everyone left in the courtroom. She then looks back up and says, "Blue is my favourite color. Thank you for dressing up to come to court. Everyone else should have done like you." Yep! A blue suit and white shirt; that Holy Spirit unction me to wear got my case dismissed. This wasn't something that I had studied or planned for. It was revealed to me. Holy Spirit knew the attitude of the judge and what would cause her to act in more of a calm way. And because I listened, not that I was special, I listened, and favour abounded.

A Kingdom LEADer has an advancing life advantage. Advance means *to move forward in a purposeful way, to progress or gain ground.* Kingdom LEADers should not just operate. The job of a LEADer is to cause others to move forward purposefully, progress, and gain ground. But this comes with the LEADership partnering of Holy Spirit, ... *while the Lord kept working with them and confirming the message by the attesting signs and miracles that closely accompanied [it]. Amen (so be it)* (Mark 16:20 AMPC). Kingdom LEADers have an open door into a person's spirit, so the position should not be taken lightly or alone. By alone, I mean with your intellect and skill only, *For what knows the things of a man, save the spirit of man which is in him? Even so the things of God knows no man, the Spirit of God* (I Corinthians 2:11). There are enough secular LEADers. God wants those with whom He has called to LEAD with His Spirit and not by theirs, *And my message and my preaching were very plain. Rather than using clever and persuasive speeches,* **I relied only on the power of the Holy Spirit.** *5 I did this so you would trust not in human wisdom but in the power of God* (I Corinthians 2:4-5 NLT).

As a LEADer, where are you LEADing from? Is it a dependence upon the Spirit of God, thus pushing people to the One you rely on? Or is your LEADership strategy likened unto those of the secular, that hook the people into being followers and dependent upon them? If you focus on advancing the people through the LEADing of the Spirit, you will automatically advance. *And I will make of you a great nation, and I will bless you [with abundant increase of favors] and make your name famous and distinguished, and you will be a blesssing [dispensing good to others]* (Genesis 12:2AMPC). And in doing so, prove that you can be trusted with the hidden wisdom of God.

| Chapter 5

Clarity of the Assignment

"I knew you before you were formed within your mother's womb; before you were born, I sanctified you and appointed you as my spokesman to the world."
Jeremiah 1:5

Paul

The apostle Paul was clear on what his assignment was. I believe that this is where much of his boldness came from. Would it be safe to consider that Paul had such depth of revelation of the Word of God because he was clear on who he was assigned to and what he was assigned to do, *To reveal (unveil, disclose) His Son within me so that I might proclaim Him among the Gentiles (the non-Jewish world) as the glad tidings (Gospel), immediately I did not confer with flesh and blood [did not consult or counsel with any frail human being or communicate with anyone] (Galatians 1:15-16).* By knowing his assignment, Paul could easily rule out what he should and should not be doing and recognize God's voice when He was speaking to him because he could juxtapose the voice with the assignment.

From Paul's Lead

We gain from Paul's LEAD that effective LEADership can only happen when you are clear on what you should be LEADing in. Just because you are good at doing something does not mean that you are called to it, *All things are lawful for me, but all things are not expedient, all things are lawful or me, but all things edify not* (I Corinthians 10:23). You are not assigned to meet every need that arises, and you are not assigned to everybody.

Clarity of The Assignment

Purpose is the greatest discovery for a man - knowing the reason for which you were put here on earth. I call this the big "why" question. We have all been given an assignment in life, and we have been prebuilt to achieve that particular assignment; *your eyes saw my unformed substance, and in Your book all the days [of my life] were written before ever they took shape, when as yet there was none of them* (Psalm 139:16 AMPC).

Your assignment must be discovered. You were not created to live your life hitting and missing. You have been given something that fits your character, your mind can process it fluidly, and you have joy and fulfilment in doing it. Everyone, even if they have a physical deficiency, has an assignment and the ability to achieve it. Unfortunately, in today's society, people are positioned and chosen based on their ability to draw crowds. People seek after things for the financial benefit or the one with the most influence. Society does not look for people who are gifted and assigned to that area of need, so we often have people in positions who do not have the expertise, knowledge, or skillset to complete the task, add value or solve the problem. The other ironic thing is that Kingdom LEADers have given adherence to this same form of operation for fear of being left out or behind. But a Kingdom LEADer does not have to worry about that. No assignment from God will return void or become inactive on the earth unless the LEADer themselves are not active in it.

> God doesn't limit the success to the size of the assignment.

When a LEADer is active in what God has assigned them to do, they come outfitted with mental fortitude and the spiritual mantle to handle any matter; natural or spiritual, that may occur. What often happens is that LEADers are found fighting battles and dealing with spiritual matters that are outside of their assignment, and incur setbacks and failure for doing something that they were not assigned to do, to begin with; b*ut we will not boast of things without our measure, but according to the measure of the rule which God hath distributed to us, a measure to reach even unto you* (II Corinthians 10:13).

God has dealt to every man a measure of faith (Romans 12:3). Within that measure of faith lies your assignment on the earth and the way in which God chose to funnel purpose, potential, and prosperity to you. Also, within that measure, LEADers will have a different administration and a diverse way in which they operate, *And there are differences of administrations, but the same Lord. 6 And there are diversities of operations, but it is the same God which worketh all in all* (I Corinthians 12:5-6). This is what sets each LEADer's assignment apart from the other. Peter was an apostle assigned to the Jews. Paul was also an apostle but assigned to the Gentiles. Both had the same measure of faith, which was to carry the message of the Gospel of the Kingdom, but their differences and administration changed based on the people to whom they were individually called to. *We, however, will not boast beyond proper limits, but will confine our boasting to the sphere of service God Himself has assigned to us, a sphere that also includes you* (II Corinthians 10:13 NIV). You have an "in-particular," way in which you will carry out your assignment - your way.

You are not here to simply exist. You should not just find something to do. **You should be building yourself in your assignment**, and that assignment is critical to your life success and the lives of others, *"The Spirit of the Lord is upon Me, for He has anointed Me to bring Good News to the poor. He has sent Me to proclaim that captives will be released, that the blind will see, that the oppressed will be set free, 19 and that the time of the Lord's favor has come"* (Luke 4:18-19 NLT). You are anointed for something. To be outside of an assignment is to be outside of what you have been anointed to do. It is dangerous being outside of the assignment. You have to fight your way to the top when you are outside of the assignment, because you are outside of your element. You are doing versus being because you are like the fish out of the water. The movement doesn't change, but it has lost its fluidity because it's not in the environment it was designed for. But when you are inside your assignment, the same movement that we call flapping out of the water is swimming in the water - the right environment.

Have you discovered your assignment? The reason this is so important is because every assignment has its challenges. But with each challenge comes an in-built ability to handle it. You are buillt for it! On the contrary, if you are not in your assignment and you are doing something because it seems to give you an advantage, you are soon destined for a setback because you are not built for the challenges that come along with that assignment. I get asked all the time, "How do I handle being a pastor and people?" My only reply is that I am built for it. My wife cannot understand. She said she would lose her mind. I understand that it's because she isn't built for what I do. On the other hand, she handles the ministry's administrative side, and I think I would lose my mind. But because we are doing what we have been prewired and built to do, what looks difficult to others is a breeze for us. A lot like seeing a fish swimming in the water and flapping out of it. Which, in reality, the fish is actually only trying to swim. The flapping would be the same movement in the water.

Trapped in Another Assignment

But God's amazing grace has made me who I am! And his grace to me was not fruitless. In fact, I worked harder than all the rest, yet not in my own strength but God's, for his empowering grace is poured out upon me.
I Corinthians 15:10TPT

You should only do what you have been created to do. Many LEADers are trapped in another work because they did not take the time to discover what their assignment was. *Man's goings are of the Lord; how can a man then understand his own way* (Proverbs 20:24)? There is a difference between a good thing and a God thing. What Kingdom LEADers should want to be in is the God thing. The God thing keeps you from being trapped in an assignment that you do not belong to. So often, LEADers don't see the growth or provision that they desire, but it's because God does not misplace resources. The plan of God has an expected end. <u>The assignment **for your life** has been processed through Alpha and Omega</u>. Any other assignment has not gone through that process because God did not see you in it. So, God saw no need to provide for you anything other than a way of escape. LEADers must become positively persuaded by what God has called them to do. You have been given assignment boldness, strength, grace, perseverance, help, and faith to accomplish everything your assignment will entail. That faith is designed to work for you every time. But what it is not designed to do is work in an area that you have not been given the assignment or call to abide in, *For we stretch not ourselves beyond our measure, as though we reached not unto you: for we are come as far as to you also in preaching the Gospel of Christ* (II Corinthians 10:14).

> Avoid the trap of needing to do many things. Find the one thing and do it right.

You have all the freedom of the lane that you're assigned to. Find the thing that you are assigned to do, and do it well. Resist being common - be EXCEPTIONAL! Never assume that the ones who are doing a lot are on assignment. Sometimes, more is needed to cover the wrong that shouldn't be done. Truthfully speaking, they should not be the object that stands in the way of your progress. When you LEAD from your position of assignment, you have everything you need and are assured of operating at your best because you are doing the very thing that you were anointed and assigned to do. **Fads and trends come and go, but assignment is long-lasting.** Being built within assignment is the ability to hold up against the changing of times, the shifting of culture, and the passing of generations.

Run Your Race

... and let us **run** with patient endurance *and* steady *and* active persistence **the appointed course of the race** that is set before us.
Hebrews 12:1 AMPC

Yet **grace** (God's unmerited favor) **was given to each of us individually** [not indiscriminately, but **in different ways**] in proportion to the measure of Christ's [rich and bounteous] gift.
Ephesians 4:7 AMPC

Every LEADer has his or her own race to run. You cannot win a race that you were not gifted to run in. A few things come to mind when I say, "Run your race." In track and field, each runner has their own lane. If they cross over into someone else's lane, they foul out. The LEADers must be careful not to be in a lane they were not given. They will not be at their best; they abandon the grace bestowed upon them for the race, their uniqueness goes unnoticed, and their gift is muzzled, all because they are not LEADing as they have been assigned. This is so important because it even relates to how we have been built; spiritually, physically, mentally, and socially. You are an investment sent from Heaven. Pre-engineered. And **you have been fabricated by the hand of God to do a particular thing and do it well. It's your genius**, *For we are God's [own] handiwork (His workmanship), recreated in Christ Jesus, [born anew] that we may do those good works which God predestined (planned beforehand) for us [taking paths which He prepared ahead of time], that we should walk in them [living the good life which He prearranged and made ready for us to live]* (Ephesians 2:10 AMPC). Did you notice that the scripture said **that we should walk in them**? I call this the "protective clause of God" that you will often find in scripture, where God says that He has done something for His creation. It's necessary because we believe that it will happen automatically just because God said it. But this is not so. The Word of God must be acted upon. So, if you don't see what God said, it does not mean that God did not provide it. You just chose to do something different than what He planned.

> In Christ, winning is in every lane.

LEADer, you are the workmanship of God. It has been divinely predestined and planned, and you have been divinely placed to succeed, increase, and live a good life. But it's in the lane that you have been assigned to run.

The other thing I thought of as it pertains to Run Your Race was the 1 talent servant in Matthew 25. Because of his perception of the talent, he went and hid it. What the false perception did not allow him to see was that there was more talent in the talent if it was simply put in the right environment. He hid it in the ground rather than putting the talent to work. His lord said, *...you should have invested my money with the bankers, and at my coming I would have received what was my own with interest* (Matthew 25:27 AMPC). The story concludes with the servant losing the talent he did have and being cast out into a workforce that was painstaking and rigorous (Matthew 25:27-30). Had he only worked on the talent and not buried it.

This is the condition of many LEADers who aren't running their race. They aren't working their talent. They are caught up in someone else's. This is happening in every sphere of life. People have not settled on what God has given them and how God has given them to do it. In essence, they have buried their talent. In Christ, winning is in every lane and on every talent.

| Chapter 6

Confidence in God's Ability

Being confident of this very thing, that he which hath begun a good work in you will perform it until the day of Jesus Christ.
Philippians 1:6

David

What confidence is in a 12-year-old boy to take a sling and four stones in his handbag and run towards a giant named Goliath when an entire army refuses to fight him? It wasn't just confidence in his ability. It was confidence in who was fighting for him, *Then said David to the Philistine, Thou comest to me with a sword, and with a spear, and with a shield: but I come to thee in the Name of the Lord of Hosts, the God of the Armies of Israel, whom thou hast defied* (I Samuel 17:45). This same David testified that he slew a lion and a bear and this uncircumcised Philistine shall be one of them, seeing he hath defied the armies of the living God.

And out of the mouth of David lies the secret sauce to confidence. It's not in our ability; it is in God's. A LEADer should always remain dependent on the ability of the one fighting. David never approached the fight with his own strength or ability. He was 12. But God working through a 12-year-old made him bigger than the giant, *"not by might nor by power, but by My Spirit," saith the Lord of Hosts* (Zechariah 4:6c). Goliath saw a kid, but the kid saw God fighting for him. And he did not need the stature or strength of the giant; he only needed confidence n God's ability, *but the people that do know their God shall be strong, and do exploits* (Daniel 11:32).

From David's Lead

Confidence is a size-, skill-, or performance-based skill. It is a matter of knowing who called you and what you are capable of achieving when you are in partnership with the Lord of Hosts. David had confidence in what he was fighting because he was confident in the one fighting with him.

Confidence in God's Ability

As LEADer, you must have confidence. Not just in you but in God working in you, through you, and for you. Your confidence carries great compensation (Hebrews 10:35.) Often, confidence can be misconstrued as being conceded. But though they may look the same, they are on opposite ends of the spectrum. A conceded person isn't reliant upon God's ability. They are showboating in the ability that God has given them. But a confident person, they rest in the arms of a godly confidence as they do the work, and walk in the footprints of a path that they are anointed to travel.

> There is a uniqueness that only you and only you can give. That uniqueness is also here your anointing lies.

When Right Way started, we were in a school foyer. We went from the foyer to the library, and from the library to the gym, which became our home for five years. I had a pastor that reached out to me and wanted to talk. We ended up meeting me in the Office Depot parking lot. When he approached me, he first said that he wanted to repent. He said that he thought that I was the most conceded pastor he had ever seen. Then he said, I was wrong. He had prayed to God for help, and God told him to come and talk with me. He then said something that was shocking. Now, mind you, we are in a school gym having church. I'm frustrated because those 5 years were hard. The cleaning, setting up, and breaking down of equipment. The pastor asked, "How do you do it?" He continued, "I'm in a church building, and you are in a gym, packing it out, and I can't get fifty people to come." What's the secret? He asked. First off, I needed to hear that. A poart of me was thinking that I wasn't doing anything. Yet from the outside looking in, people are seeing a packed gym on Sundays by this preacher and want to know what it is that has people coming to a gym to get the Word.

I then began to ask the pastor what he was currently doing. I heard a few right things and a lot of wrong things. But the one thing that kept coming up was his replication of what other pastors and churches were doing. I told him that he had the wrong focus. I told Him that vision comes from God, not man, and challenged him on whether he even prayed about his actions. I then asked him several questions:

1. **What is your anointing?** Meaning, what has God anointed you to teach? What message has God given you to give? What have you been endowed to do? And have you studied and been equipped enough in it to teach, do, or relay it by heart?

He was doing what everyone was doing, but he was not doing what he was anointed to do, the way he was anointed to do it, *And there are differences of administrations, but the same Lord. 6 And there are diversities of operations, but it is the same God which worketh all in all* (I Corinthians 12:4-5).

2. **Who are you called to?** Are you even working with the right bait? *For so hath the Lord commanded us, saying, I have set thee to be a light of the Gentiles, that thou shouldest be for salvation unto the ends of the earth. 48 And when the Gentiles heard this, they were glad, and glorified the word of the Lord: and as many as were ordained to eternal life believed. 49 And the word of the Lord was published throughout all the region* (Acts 13:47-49).

Don't be a Walmart if that's not your calling. You do not have to fall into the trap of trying to be everything to everyone, *For we* **stretch not ourselves beyond our measure** (II Corinthians 10:14a).

3. **Are you confident in who you are?** This is the one that most LEADers struggle with, as did this pastor. Everyone wants to jump on the next big thing or something that seems to work for someone else. And just because it's working for them doesn't mean it will work for you. I shared with him that **one of my rules is that I've got to be me and do things my way**. I discovered this revelation from Paul where he said the same thing, just with different verbiage, *But by the grace of God* **I am what I am**: *and His grace which* **was bestowed upon me** *was not in vain; but I laboured more abundantly than they all: yet not I, but the grace of God which was with me* (I Corinthians 15:10).

This pastor's eyes lit up when I asked that. I think he saw what the problem was at that moment because, for years, he had been copying this famous pastor's moves and wasn't getting the same result. Actually, he admitted to losing people and money and seeing no growth in his church. This is where it was troubling to him because he had an actual church building while I was renting a school gymnasium and did not seem to have that problem. After a few more words, we prayed. I gave him some ministry tools that would help him become who he needed to be.

There is a grace on every LEADer that is tailored specifically for them. If I could just get this one point across to LEADers, it would make all the other chapters in this book make sense. **Once you know your know; the presence of God, the voice of Holy Spirit, the relationship with Christ, and the confidence to do it your way become much more appreciated.** You see things differently. When a LEADer mimics someone else, they rob themselves of the differentness that God has equipped them with, as was the case with this pastor. He was looking at what other famous pastors were doing and, without knowing it, attempting to copy the same pattern, hoping to get the same results, but it was not working for him.

This is the thing that made him think that I that conceded. The mere fact that I was settled in doing it my way - the way God designed me to function and be. But it was confidence. **You need confidence in your ability to do what God has given you to do**. See, it's not hard being you; you just have to make that discovery. And this isn't just a LEADer's attribute. **Everyone needs to know their know**. When a person replicates someone else, they communicate to God that they are displeased with who and how He designed them. See, it costs you to copy. You rob yourself of authenticity and exert energy in an unneeded area, whereas being you comes naturally. **Being who you were called and created to be only requires acceptance and confidence.** It may not be the best for others, but it is what's best for you. It may not be a fit for others, but it most certainly fits you. I will not attract everyone, but you can rest assured that everything God designs, He designed for success. When we are living with confidence in God's ability, we are operating out of the fullness of God's ability, *Now when they saw the boldness of Peter and John, and perceived that they were unlearned and ignorant men, they marvelled; and they took knowledge of them, that they had been with Jesus* (Acts 4:13).

A Know

Confidence comes out of your know. I believe that this is a major key to dynamic LEADership. There is a LEADership style that you have been gifted with. It is a thing that God intends for you to build and expand upon. A message and a way that you have been gifted in doing. It should flow out of you with ease. The issue arises when a LEADer sees another LEADer in their know, and it seems to be more attractive and productive than what they have been given, and they abandon their know, *For we dare not make ourselves of the number, or compare ourselves with some that commend themselves: but they measuring themselves by themselves, and comparing themselves among themselves, are not wise* (II Corinthians 10:12). **You have to do it the way you have been given to do it**. *And Saul armed David with his armour, and he put an helmet of brass upon his head; also he armed him with a coat of mail. [39] <u>And David girded his sword upon his armour</u>, and he assayed to go; for he had not proved it. **And David said unto Saul, I cannot go with these; for I have not proved them**. <u>And David put them off him</u>. [40] And he* *took his staff in his hand, and chose him five smooth stones out of the brook, and put them in a shepherd's bag which he had, even in a scrip; and his sling was in his hand: and he drew near to the* Philistine (I Samuel 17:38-40).

There is so much to unpack in those scriptures. It shows why so many LEADers fail. They are armed the wrong way and wearing things that aren't proven for them. They don't see what they have been given as being good enough to accomplish the task at hand because the task looks bigger than what they have to work with. But what has been given to you (you know) is capable of accomplishing the task, or else you would not have been given it. This is a powerful revelation. Because **in the know that God has given you, He has tucked Himself in it to work in and through you that way. Therefore, when you abandon your uniqueness, you abandon God's way of operating in you. You are also stretching yourself outside of your capability.** So instead of a flow, there is strain, unneeded pressure, and a delusion of a need to perform rather than the motivation of fulfilment.

How has God uniquely crafted you to operate? What is the message that you carry? Not one that you have to go and get. God has given you the grace to do something special. There is a burning on the inside of you right now, and that burn has to turn into passion and excitement for you, *But **by the grace of God, I am what I am***: *and His grace which was bestowed upon me was not in vain; but I laboured more abundantly than they all: yet not I, but the* *grace of God which was with me* (I Corinthians 15:10). Too often, LEADers discredit themselves and what they have been given. Not every grace is called to a huge crowd or a huge stage. But this does not invalidate the call. **The blessing is not in the crowd or on the stage. The blessing is in the know.** I wish every LEADer would discover this before they set out to LEAD. It will shed light on so many things. Just the know alone will keep the LEADer from merging into lanes that are not a part of their LEADrship. It will save them from being distracted by things that don't add value to their know. It will even keep them from becoming envious and jealous of the growth and success of other LEADers. It kills competition and compels completion. It empowers the LEADer with boldness to simply be themselves, do what they have been called to do, and LEAD by their designed assignment.

You have something special! **The know is the God-factor in you**, *But we have this treasure in earthen vessels, that the excellency of the power may be of God, and not of us* (II Corinthians 4:7). It is designed *to <u>make room</u> for you and <u>before the great it LEADeth him</u>* (Proverbs 18:16YLT). **Quite often, success is missed because the know is absent.** Find your know, accept it, work it, and watch your LEADership style grow.

| Chapter 7

Humility

> LEADer Note:
> **Wear Humility like a rob.**

... Yea, all of you be subject one to another, and be clothed with humility: for God resisteth the proud, and giveth grace to the humble.
I Peter 5:5b

Humility is one of the greatest characteristics of a LEADer. Unfortunately, it has the greatest potential of being overlooked. As I mentioned in an earlier Chapter, most LEADers are being served. Many LEADers are having people meeting their needs. I want to pause by saying I believe that it is so important that LEADers know what it is like to serve another before being served themselves. Jesus said that *anyone who wants to be first, the same should be last and servant of all* (Mark 9:35). One of our current problems is that we have LEADers that have never served another, so they have never had an encounter with the work of humility. Thus, we have to teach LEADers something they should have experienced on their way to becoming a LEADer themselves. This entire book is actually written for this reason. **As a LEADer, you never move out of the positional action of servant**. I see myself as a servant-LEADer. The moment you miss the servanthood in LEADing, you move from being humble to haughty and needing to be humbled. *People with a big head are headed for a fall, pretentious egos brought down a peg* (Isaiah 2:11 MSG). Humility protects the LEADers and keeps the LEADer from becoming prideful and arrogant. The danger of LEADing is that although it's serving, it puts you in the spotlight and gives the view of it being about you. When you add to that the congratulations and praise from the people, policing the fascination is vitally important so that you do not become lured into pride and taking the glory that belongs to God for self. Humility is the gatekeeper, *You must have the same attitude that Christ Jesus had. ⁶ Though He was God, He did not think of equality with God as something to cling to. ⁷ Instead, He gave up His divine privileges, He took the humble position of a slave and was born as a human being. When He appeared in human form, ⁸* **He humbled Himself in obedience to God** *and died a criminal's death on a Cross* (Philippians 2:5-8 NLT).

It was serving faithfully that brought me to where I am. Those beginnings are what keep me humble. And even today, as a Senior Pastor, I look for the opportunity to serve. I walk the Church grounds and pick up paper. I help move tables. And although they come up and take it away from me, I never want to unintentionally take on an improper outlook on myself. I want the people to always know that it is by the grace of God that I LEAD. **It is important that the LEADer wear humility like a robe.** It's their greatest safeguard. It is not something you put on or take off. You wear it all the time.

Humility's Posture

The posture of humility is that of you serving up. Up to the people, not down to them. This is why being a LEADer demands humility. The position alone does not put you there, so a LEADer must ensure they are policing themselves in this area. It is often said that the higher you go up, the more responsible people see you. But in all truth, the higher you go, the less responsible people see you because, in their minds, it was your responsibility that got you there. And although LEADers should become more responsible, many don't. Humility is what keeps the obligation of being responsible in place. As a pastor, I always remind myself that these are God's people, and I have no right to treat them in any kind of way. And even if they do wrong to me, God is holding me accountable and responsible for my actions to them.

> Nothing protects the LEADer from pride like the posture of humility.

There is nothing more demeaning than a prideful LEADer. *A man's pride shall bring him low: but honour shall uphold the humble in spirit* (Proverbs 29:23). If you see a prideful LEADer, it is because they have allowed the position to reach their head. **LEADer is a heart position.**

Somewhere they lost sight of what it means to LEAD and what it means to be humble. See, **a leader is not only LEADing with what they say, but they are also leading even more with what they do**. People mimic what they see more than what they hear. Action and interaction speak more than you will ever know. **Humility says I am a servant to you.** Humility always asks, "What can I do for you." **Any LEADer looking for honour must go through humility to get it**. There is no other true way. *Fear of the Lord teaches wisdom, humility precedes honor* (Proverbs 15:3 NLT). And if a LEADer wants to stay being honoured, they have to stay walking in humility, *Humble yourselves in the sight of the Lord, and He shall lift you up* (James 4:10). Humility is an amazing guiding force.

What I have learned simply through the eye of humility is astounding. Many LEADers want to exude wisdom. But the one thing that should exude from the Kingdom LEADer is humility. It plays a direct role in how they handle people. Humility causes you to see the best in people. **LEADers who don't like people lack humility**. Imagine if God were tired of you. Humility is that spiritual reminder that you don't have it all together and did not and still do not get it right all the time, so it reassures you in the persistent extending of grace and mercy.

This attribute of humility cannot be stressed enough. LEADers work on how they look, their pontification, the growth of their gifts, making themselves knowledgeable of subject matters, and many other contributing factors.

But how many LEADers make humility their focus of concern? Many LEADers started out so close and now have moved so far away. Does the position of LEADing need that distance of protection from the people, or have LEADers become insensitive to how to LEAD? Have they lost the humility that they started out with? See, when most LEADers start out, they have to be humble. It was enforced upon them. But **the true perception of humility becomes apparent in your posture once you are in the LEAD**. This is when the LEADer has to humble themselves.

The one thing that will safeguard the LEADer in this area of humility is worship. The moving away often starts at the place of worship. The LEADer can never be too busy, and the worship moment is not a factor. Worship is a protector. It keeps the heart postured towards God and the mind reflective of His goodness. It points to Him as the source and you as the conduit through which His gifts and abilities work. It is acknowledging God's worth. So, when the LEADer doesn't worship, they shelve the worth of God in what they do. And where worship is absent, humility is negated.

The worship component is important because with LEADership comes with a crowing. This is an authority for guiding and directing people. Worship is the place of humbling, whereby the LEADer brings that crowning authority and casts it at the feet of Jesus. If there is one thing that I am most constant about, it is worship and thanksgiving. It is the most humbling thing because, as I said in an earlier chapter, LEADing has you upfront. And although your heart intends never to usurp God's authority, if there is nothing to guard against that, Satan will slowly sift you into pride. Worship is that defence against that ever happening.

Jesus

The One who came to save, redeem, and restore, and through whom all would be saved, demonstrated the greatest display of humility by girding Himself and washing the feet of the disciples. Not only that, but He was found amongst the publicans and sinners. Jesus told them to follow Him as we do, but His display of LEADership was lived out in His humility. The Bible says that *He thought it no robbery to consider Himself to be equal with God, but made Himself of no reputation and became a servant.* It was this act of humility that *raised Him up and gave Him a name that was higher than any other name* (Philippians 2:5-11). This isn't strange. It is actually the same principle that He not only taught the disciples, but also led in demonstration, *"Whoever wants to be first must take last place and be the servant of everyone else"* (Mark 9:35b).

This humility component is an important one. Though in charge, it positions the LEADer beside those with whom they are LEADing and communicates togetherness and oneness. If any LEADer is struggling with garrisoning and unifying those that they are LEADing, they should examine their attitude through humility.

| Chapter 8

Faithful

Moreover, **it is** [essentially] **required of stewards** that a man should be found faithful [proving himself worthy of trust].
I Corinthians 4:2 AMPC

Job

If there is anyone we can draw from concerning faithfulness, it would be Job. Imagine having all your children die at once and losing everything you have, and your wife suggests that you curse God and die, and your response is, *"blessed be the Name of the Lord"* (Job 1:21). The Bible even goes on to say that *"in all this Job sinned not, nor charged God foolishly"* (Job 1:22). Job remained faithful. He remained loyal and steadfast.

Just imagine what Job's life looked like in the presence of others. You go from having it all and being known as the blameless, upright man in Uz to losing it all. Everyone who once had a relationship with you abandons you. Not because God said so, but because of what his life looked like. Surely his life looked cursed to others, and even his friends, with their unwarranted advice, suggested that he must have done something against God that landed him in that condition. But neither abandonment nor blame caused Job to return from his commitment to serving God faithfully.

From Job's Lead

Job shows us what it takes to be a faithful LEADer. There will be times when things are in total opposition to what the Word of God says. There are going to be times when things and even people are not pulling for you. But the questionable decision becomes: Do you believe and are you committed to staying faithful to the call when it does not look like the call at all? Job did not allow a disruption and loss in a situation to change his dedication to God. And because of his resolute decision to remain faithful in an unforeseen moment, Job's faithfulness paid off in the end. ***And the Lord turned the captivity of Job***, *when he prayed for his friends: also the Lord gave Job twice as much as he had before.* **11** *Then came there unto him all his brethren, and all his sisters, and all they that had been of his acquaintance before, and did eat bread with him in his house: and they bemoaned him, and comforted him over all the evil that the Lord had brought upon him: every man* *also gave him a piece of money, and every one an earring of gold. 12 So the Lord blessed the latter end of Job more than his beginning: for he had fourteen thousand sheep, and six thousand camels, and a thousand yoke of oxen, and a thousand she asses. 13 He had also seven sons and three daughters. 14 And he called the name of the first, Jemima; and the name of the second, Kezia; and the name of the third, Keren-happuch 15 And in all the land were no women found so fair as the daughters of Job: and their father gave them inheritance among their brethren. 16 After this lived Job an hundred and forty years, and saw his sons, and his sons' sons, even four generations. 17 So Job died, being old and full of days.*

Faithful

In the hand of the LEADer is one of the most precious things to Jesus: the Church/His Bride/people. And what God wants from LEADership is the ability to be faithful, even in hard times. This is important because LEADers are God's heart to the people. They stand as representatives of God to the people. The people are to *follow those who, through faith and patience, inherit the promise.* But if from the LEADer comes unfaithfulness and untrustworthiness, then that has the ability to shed a negative reflection on God. LEADers are supposed to remain faithful to God and His Word at all costs. Job lost it all, but he did not allow that to move him from being faithful to God.

There is so much happening in the church world. There are people who want to have very little to do with the Church because of LEADership. It is not that they don't want God. Oftentimes, LEADers cause people to have a negative outlook on the Church. But when faithfulness exists, there is a decision to remain loyal and steadfast no matter what comes your way. A LEADer remembers their "Yes, Lord," when there was no one and not much. So now, more people and more things don't change who they are because faithfulness in the least warrants the LEADer to be the ruler over the much.

I believe that this is why the Bible tells us not to despise small beginnings (Zechariah 4:10), because it is in these times that the skill of faithfulness is being developed in the heart. If you are mishandling five, you will surely mishandle five hundred.

Faithfulness is an essential asset for an effective LEADer. I am willing to go out on a limb by saying we can judge the future success of the LEADer by examining how faithful they are in the small things. Luke 16:10-12 says, *He that is faithful in that which is least is faithful also in much: and he that is unjust in the least is unjust also in much. 11 If therefore ye have not been faithful in the unrighteous mammon, who will commit to your trust the true riches? 12 And if ye have not been faithful in that which is another man's, who shall give you that which is your own?* **The true test of promotion is faithfulness**. This asset is often overlooked because man often promotes based on skill or performance. And this is why we see so many people in the church who perform well but lack commitment and perseverance. **Skill alone is a worldly way of LEADing. With God, faithfulness is the grade that elevates you,** *And if you are not faithful with other people's things, why should you be trusted with things of your own?* (Luke 16:12 NLT)

I served my former pastor faithfully. I oversaw the East location of the Church for two years. At the same time, I was also the youth pastor. I managed his TV station, wrote scripts, produced, and edited shows. God then calls me to start my own Church. We spent the first five years in school, from the front foyer to the library and finally to the school gymnasium. I remember the unfair days of scrubbing floors and cleaning the entire gym when it was the school's responsibility to have it cleaned. We were walking the campus to pick up trash because, to me, on Sundays, it was the Lord's house, and it had to look its best. Driving around the neighbourhood on Friday to put up church signs for service on Sunday and then having to round them up after service. I drove a single-cab Dodge truck that my uncle let us borrow because we lost our car. Imagine five people (two adults and three kids) in a single-cab standard-shift truck. But in all that, we were faithful, even to my kids. As small as they were, they were hands-on. So today, when people see how we live and what we drive, I am very clear that it didn't come from performance; this is our reward for our faithfulness.

We have been using the Word 'faithful,' but this word is synonymous with trustworthy, dependable, reliable, constant, and honourable. **Real LEADers are faithful**! It's a quality that you don't just teach, you LEAD with it. You should always strive to do and be your best, *but a faithful man shall abound in blessing* (Proverbs 28:20). The servant was not awarded being ruler over much because of how well he performed. The ruler over much came from being faithful over a few (Matthew 5:23).

Are you a faithful LEADer? Not just when everything is going well, but in the crucibles of life, because that's when faithfulness steps up and really answers the call. To your care, God has entrusted the single most precious thing to Him - the Church. He was faithful to the death of the Cross to get her back, and now He is holding you accountable, LEADer, to be faithful in stewarding her.

| Chapter 9
Spiritual Accountability

LEADer Note:
You are checking on everyone else, who are you checking in with?

And the apostles gathered themselves together unto Jesus, and told Him all things, both what they had done, and what they had taught.
Mark 6:30

The Apostles

And the apostles **gathered themselves together** *unto Jesus, and* **told Him all things, both what they had done, and what they had taught**. Even the apostles had spiritual accountability. They are anointed to heal the sick, cast out devils, and sent to preach the Gospel of the Kingdom, and yet they still held themselves accountable to someone other than themselves. They are also reporting on what was done and what they taught. We can even see accountability in how Jesus sent the apostles out. He told them to go out *two by two* (Luke 10:1). We do not find in scripture under the New

103

Testament where the LEADers moved independently of themselves, *and when Saul came to Jerusalem, <u>he assayed</u>* **to join himself to the disciples,** *and* **he was with them** *coming and going out at Jerusalem* (Acts 9:26,28). We also see God commisioning both Paul and Barnabus as a team (Acts 13:1-4).

From The Apostles

We learn from the apostles that having been given authority does not free a person from being held accountable by authority. It is in the best interest and protection of the LEADer that they hold themselves accountable to someone else. Our Lord and Saviour Himself testifled that He was accountable to the Father, *So Jesus said, "When you have lifted up the Son of Man on the Cross, then you will understand that I am He. I do nothing on My own but say only what the Father taught Me* (John 8:28NLT).

Spiritual Authority

LEADers are often found out front; LEADing, building, and checking on the wellbeing of others. But who has the LEADer submitted and made themselves accountable to? We were not designed to completely watch over ourselves. When you make yourself accountable to someone, you are exercising accountability and putting around you a safeguard. *Where no counsel is, the people fall: but in the multitude of counsellor there is safety* (Proverbs 11:14).

There has to be someone with whom you give the freedom to speak into your life. Someone that is in prayer for your well-being. Someone that you can be naked in front of concerning your weaknesses and inner struggles, *admit your faults to one another and pray for each other so that you may be healed. The earnest prayer of a righteous man has great power and wonderful results* (James 5:16 TLB). LEADers often look over the need of this person in their lives, but this relationship provides huge benefits. See, you have to put sin (weaknesses) in the light. You cannot just know about it yourself. You have to be willing to let someone other than just you into that space. The more the LEADer hides and shelters it, the more dangerous it becomes of overtaking them. I heard someone say that **we are only as sick as our secrets**. When you get it into the light, it loses its power. And you have someone who will always stay on the wall for your success and mastering of it. I say master because we all will have something in our lives while in this body, that the deliverance will come through our dependence on God's strength in that area, *For this thing I besought the Lord thrice, that it might depart from me. 9 And He said unto me, My grace is sufficient for thee: for My strength is made perfect in weakness. Most gladly therefore will I rather glory in my infirmities, that the power of Christ may rest upon me* (II Corinthians 12:8-9).

> You are not designed to see all of you. You need someone who you will permit to see the vulnerable areas of your life.

The position of LEADing can often hide the LEADer from themselves. This is why spiritual accountability is important. Your gifts and talents aren't given to you for you. They are God-given to you for others. For instance, I cannot pastor myself. **There is a necessity for the LEADer to have someone to look up to, just as others are looking up to them**. This becomes one of the greatest deceptions of the LEADer. Because LEADers are able to answer the problems of others, they believe that they have also been empowered and equipped for themselves. This is a danger zone for the LEADer. The LEADer has to see the value of accountability, or else they are setting themselves, their goals, their success, and their future up for sabotage. Someone has to be given the permission to look within and speak into your life.

The downfall of many famous and once notable persons was often because they had no one to whom they permitted and committed themselves to being accountable to. They often paid all the bills, had fame, and for the most part, they were the ones that the others looked to, so they listened to no one. Had they only valued and regarded the relationship of accountability, many would possibly be alive and still LEADing well today. *Two people are better off than one, for they can help each other succeed. 10 If one person falls, the other can reach out and help. But someone who falls alone is in real trouble* (Ecclesiastes 4:9-10 NLT). So, we can also say that accountability bids for humility because accountability demands that you become humble to someone else's partnering role in the LEADing of your life. It's the iron sharping iron principle that many avoid. When iron is sharpened iron, there is heat and friction involved. This heat and friction is not to separate the two, but it is necessary in the sharpening process. So it is when you have someone with whom you are committing to hold yourself accountable that you stay sharpened. Since they are there to help sharpen you, there will be a time of friction.

If there is never any friction, then you can't be sharpened. I'm noting this because LEADers don't recognise those who are irons in their lives, so they see the friction as toxic. The king of Israel hated Micaiah because he never prophesied good to him, only evil (I Kings 22:8). However, this was not the case. Because it opposed the king's desires, did not mean it was bad news. He did not respect and value who Micaiah was in his life. That his place in his life was to check his emotions and not agree with them, and he had to submit himself to his voice and not rebuff it. Micaiah spoke only as the Lord told him and the king didn't like the answers he received because it went against what he wanted to do. But Micaiah was for his good, the king just didn't want to hear it.

Micaiah was the king of Israel's iron. He was in his life to sharpen him with accountability, but the king could only see someone who he thought was against him. He saw an adversary. The king of Israel died because he did not listen to Micaiah's last prophesy and even punished him to prison for telling the truth; a truth that could have saved his life had he listened. Many LEADers die [not always physically, but from assignments, relationships, marriages, true connections, Godly trust, and positions,] because what they believed to be adversarial was Godly advice designed to keep them spiritually accountable.

Don't kill the person who is called into your life to be iron just because of adversarial moments. This may indicate that you lack accountability and need maturity to receive constructive criticism. *A friend loveth at all times,* **and a brother is born for adversity** (Proverbs 17:17). When I realised that the person who is my accountability was, in fact, put in myy life for that purpose, I told them, and I permitted them to speak into my life if they saw something that was wrong or if they felt that I was out of place. I have given members of my staff and some of my trussted prayer counselors the same liberty. This removed any apprehensions that they may have had about telling me something. It also gave them the spiritual permission to see into my life. It has been one of the best decisions I could have ever made because I have someone free from any hesitation about needing to say something to me that, from the onset, may not seem like good news, because I am the pastor. I also know that I have someone watching my back. If married, your spouse is the best person for this, and I believe this position should be communicated just as with a friend.

You Still Need Washing

> "No," Peter protested, "you will never ever wash my
> feet!" Jesus replied, "Unless I wash you, you won't belong
> to me." **9** Simon Peter exclaimed, "Then wash my hands
> and head as well, Lord, not just my feet!" **10** Jesus
> replied, "A person who has bathed all over does not need
> to wash, except for the feet, to be entirely clean. And you
> disciples are clean, but not all of you."
> John 13:8-10 NLT

The scripture shows Jesus explaining to Peter the need
for continual washing, though he was already clean. This
was an illustration of the continuing saving grace of
Jesus. That though salvation is instant, it is also constant.
A growing and becoming that befits salvation and a
saving maintenance that has to be well looked after, and
you cannot do it alone. Jesus told Peter that if you are not
allowing Me to wash your feet (the part of you that stays
dirty and needs continual washing), you can have no part
in Me. Here is where not only prayer, fasting, and reading
the Word play a part, but having someone you are
accountable to is also needed. **LEADers need someone
whom they can be naked before**. Someone who knows
your shortfall. Someone that you respect that can call you
to the carpet, and you trust that they see what they see
about you. This is not a covering to be resisted, but one
that you should be in pursuit of, *Confess your faults one to
another, and pray one for another, that ye may be healed.
The effectual fervent prayer of a righteous man availeth
much* (James 5:16). **[I believe sometimes LEADers
think that the title LEADer exempts us from being
accountable to the Word.]** The higher you go, the fewer

109

things are seen and can be so easily disregarded. This is the enemy's sifting tactic. And to the LEADer reading this that will respond with "I have Holy Spirit," the Bible says that we are to *bear one another's burden* (Galatians 6:2). The scripture doesn't leave it all up to Hoy Spirit. You have a blindside that you cannot see and the rearview mirror is not picking up. It takes someone who is in accountable agreement with you to see that.

You will never have it all. And if you think you do, you are already in trouble. God uniquely designed His body so that <u>we would need the care of another member</u>, *But some of our body parts don't require as much attention. Instead, God has mingled the body parts together, giving greater honor to the "lesser" members who lacked it.* **25 He has done this intentionally so that every member would look after the others with mutual concern,** *and so that there will be no division in the body* (I Corinthians 12:24-25 TPT). Do not be fooled or misguided into thinking you do not need anybody and that you are strong enough for yourself. This is Satan's trap to get you out on an island of your own. ***Two are better than one*** (Ecclesiastes 4:9-12). What the enemy wants is a LEADer isolated. Like a predator chasing its prey, he runs behind surreptitiously. And knowing that without accountability the LEADer will soon break away from the pack. Then alone and now helpless, the LEADer crumbles at their own demise of simply not choosing to stay spiritually accountable.

| Chapter 10

Integrity

Above all, set yourself apart as a model of a life nobly lived. With dignity, demonstrate integrity in all that you teach.
Titus 2:7TPT

This happens to be one of the guiding forces in my life. I have this statement that says **"People can ruin your reputation, but only you can destroy your integrity."** Integrity is defined as *a firm adherence to a code of especially moral or artistic values, incorruptibility. The state of being whole and undivided, soundness of moral character.* **Integrity is the dividing line for a Kingdom LEADer**.

Integrity is important because, who you really are, is when no one is watching. The catcher is that you can only hide that person for so long because integrity will always have the last say-so. *You can't keep your true self hidden forever; before long you'll be exposed. You can't hide behind a religious mask forever; sooner or later the mask will slip and your true face will be known. You can't whisper one thing in private and preach the opposite in public; the day's coming when those whispers will be repeated all over town* (Luke 12:2-3 MSG). **Integrity says I don't change just because it would never be found out or I could get away with it**. It's a firm adherence; undivided, *The integrity of the upright guides them, but the unfaithful are destroyed by their duplicity* (Proverbs 11:3 NIV). It is right to have a word that is integral. But the message should match the messenger. This does not mean that we are void of error or mistakes, but Kingdom LEADer are intentional about being true to themselves through LEADing and advocating to others.

Leading with Integrity

Three LEADing people in the Bible who represent great LEADership through integrity are Job, Joseph, and Daniel. They reveal the effectiveness of what LEADership can be to the one who allows integrity to guide them.

<u>Job</u>

Job 2:3,5
*And <u>the Lord said</u> unto Satan, Hast thou considered my servant Job, that there is none like him in the earth, **a perfect and an upright man, one that feareth God, and eschewed evil? and still, he holdeth fast his integrity**, although thou movedst me against him, to destroy him*

without cause. *⁵Then <u>said his wife</u> unto him,* **Dost thou still retain thine integrity?** *curse God, and die.*

Integrity does not just deal with what we do; we can do things right as we LEAD. But the true mark of integrity is what you do when things are not going how you want them to, and you could easily shift in a manner to produce a different and more favourable outcome. Not Job. Despite losing everything, God testified that he maintained his integrity. His wife then testified that it was his integrity that kept him alive. I see this as a very powerful principle as to why we don't see many of our LEADers today who were once in the spotlight. Because integrity is a keeper, let me repeat it: integrity will always have the last say. She judges the whole matter. And those who are found on the side of integrity come out victorious, as did Job (Job 42:10-16).

<u>Joseph</u>

Genesis 41:38-44

³⁸ And <u>Pharaoh said</u> unto his servants, **Can we find such a one as this is, a man in whom the Spirit of God is?** *³⁹ And <u>Pharaoh said unto Joseph</u>, Forasmuch as God hath shewed thee all this,* **there is none so discreet and wise as thou art:** *⁴⁰ <u>thou shalt be over my house</u>, and* **according unto thy word shall all my people be ruled:** *only in the throne will I be greater than thou. ⁴¹ And <u>Pharaoh said unto Joseph</u>,* **See, I have set thee over all the land of Egypt.** *⁴² And <u>Pharaoh took off his ring from his hand, and put it upon Joseph's hand, and arrayed him in vestures of fine linen, and put a gold chain about his neck;</u>*

*43 and he **made him to ride in the second chariot** which he had; and they cried before him, Bow the knee: and **he made him ruler over all the land of Egypt.** 44 And Pharaoh said unto Joseph, I am Pharaoh, and **without thee shall no man lift up his hand or foot in all the land of Egypt.***

Integrity will always have
the last say-so.

Genesis 41:55-57

*And when all the land of Egypt was famished, <u>the people cried to Pharaoh for bread: and Pharaoh said unto all the Egyptians,</u> **Go unto Joseph; what he saith to you, do.** 56 And the famine was over all the face of the earth: and **Joseph opened all the storehouses,** and sold unto the Egyptians; and the famine waxed sore in the land of Egypt. 57 And **all countries came into Egypt <u>to Joseph</u>** for to buy corn; because that the famine was so sore in all lands.*

Integrity not only spoke for Joseph but also testified to his LEADership. Pharoah acknowledged that the Spirit of God was on him and that there was no man like him. This means that integrity is seen.

Integrity will always outlast
the critics and the lie.

It is easy to get the people in your circle to speak well of you. Is your integrity seen and acknowledged by those outside your circle? Oftentimes, integrity is what wins over those who don't believe in God. Joseph had so much integrity that even when he could have slept with his master Potipher's wife, he didn't. **Integrity is a guide and protector**. It is who you are when no one is watching, even if you cannot get caught, *But Joseph refused. "Look," he told her, "<u>my master trusts me with everything in his entire household</u>. ⁹ No one here has more authority than I do. <u>He has held back nothing from me</u> except you, because you are his wife. How could I do such a wicked thing? It would be a great sin against God"* (Genesis 39:8-9).

<u>Daniel</u>

Daniel 6:1-5

*It pleased Darius to set over the kingdom an hundred and twenty princes, which should be over the whole kingdom; ² and over these three presidents; of whom Daniel was first: that the princes might give accounts unto them, and the king should have no damage. ³ <u>Then this **Daniel was preferred above the presidents and princes**, <u>because</u> **an excellent spirit was in him**</u>; and <u>the king thought</u> <u>to</u> **set him over the whole realm**. ⁴ Then <u>the presidents and princes sought to find occasion against Daniel</u> concerning the kingdom; <u>but</u> **they could find none occasion nor fault; forasmuch as he was faithful, neither was there any error or fault found in him**. ⁵ Then said these men, <u>We shall not find any occasion against this Daniel</u>, except we find it against him concerning the law of his God.*

No occasion could be found against Daniel. In other words, Daniel was the same in private as he was in public. That's integrity. **Integrity is who you are when**

no one is watching. Effective LEADing starts in the interpersonal areas of one's own life. Notice that the suffix of the word integrity is the preposition "in," which means that **integrity is not something you become in the moment but what you are all the time.**

The other thing we see concerning integrity is that it is akin to excellence and a criterion for Godly promotion. Not every LEADer is where they are because God promoted them. Some are where they are because of connection and mere association. Daniel was promoted to over 123 men because of an excellent spirit, and the king noticed this excellence. It is also worth mentioning that Joseph and Daniel's bosses served idol gods and were open to a Godly person and the principles they lived being worked in their system, *And Pharaoh said unto his servants, Can we find such a one as this is, a man in whom the Spirit of God is? 39 And Pharaoh said unto Joseph, Forasmuch as God hath shewed thee all this, there is none so discreet and wise as thou art: 40 thou shalt be over my house, and according unto thy word shall all my people be ruled: only in the throne will I be greater than thou. 41 And Pharaoh said unto Joseph, See, I have set thee over all the land of Egypt.* (Genesis 41:38-41). So it was also for Daniel, *Then king Darius wrote unto all people, nations, and languages, that dwell in all the earth; Peace be multiplied unto you. 26 I make a decree, That in every dominion of my kingdom men tremble and fear before the God of Daniel: for He is the living God, and stedfast for ever, and His Kingdom that which shall not be destroyed, and His dominion shall be even= unto the end.* (Daniel 6:25-

26). Neither of them lowered their standards, their credibility increased, they did not abate their work performance, nor did they relent in their relationship towards God. In the end, they were promoted, and it was their God that high regard was given to (Daniel 6:23-28).

Stay Protected

May integrity and honesty protect me,
for I put my hope in you.
Psalms 25:21

Nothing is worth giving up your integrity for. Keep it at all costs. It is your protection. The integrity position will often look like you are getting the short end of the stick - like you are being let down, looked over, and left out. Just remember, integrity always has the last say-so. Do not assume that things are a sign of success. All things that look good aren't God. *It's better to wait for an invitation to the head table than to be sent away in public disgrace* (Proverbs 25:7 NLT). **Success is doing what God has called you to do, the way that God called you to do it**. Things are add-ons that come from seeking first the Kingdom of God. God's way profits us well at the end.

Though the climb of integrity may take the longest route, the outcome yields a lasting return. Remember, if you have to leave integrity behind in order to get ahead, you are not getting ahead.

| Chapter 11

A Love for God's People

LEADer Note:
Lead with God's heart for people and with the
compassion of Christ in your heart.

This is My commandment, That ye love one another, as I
have loved you. [13] Greater love hath no man than this,
that a man lay down his life for his friends.
John 15:12-13

Moses

Though he often felt frustrated because of the stiffness of
the Hebrew children, what is undeniable is Moses's love
for the people. Once he accepted the task of being the
LEADer who would go and tell Pharaoh to let God's
people go, it was all brakes off. From LEADing a nation
out of captivity and over the Red Sea (Exodus 14), willing
to stand for hours to meet the needs of the people
(Exodus 18), standing in as an advocate for the people
when God would have destroyed them for rebelling to
enter Canaan (Numbers 14), getting before God to get a
Word and direction for the people, to even personally

appointing his successor before the people (Deuteronomy 31:1–8; 34:9), Moses demonstrated what it meant to be a LEADer who loved God's people. And when Moses made his own missteps, he never charged them to the people.

From Moses

The children of Israel were not the most loving, eager-to-follow, willingly submitted, and obedient group of people, even after seeing all the miracles God did through Moses. But God still had a plan for His people, and Moses was committed to the process. They constantly complained when things did not go their way. They always wanted to return to Egypt but cried to get out. They even asked to have Moses replaced. Despite all that, Moses's stayed focused on God's agenda and not the people's plight. This could only be done by staying connected to his mountain experiences. In other words, Moses reveals to us that **a love for the people can only come and be maintained through constant connection and love for God**. He shows us the power and benefits bestowed upon the LEADer who values the presence of God. The commitment to stay in God's presence postured his heart for the people.

A Love For God's People

Truthfully speaking, LEADing has its challenges. But one of the main keys to effective LEADership is where you LEAD from. You cannot LEAD solely on intellect; we have learned that LEADership isn't performance-based. **LEADers should do everything with their hearts and mind on God's heart and mind**. You can't LEAD effectively with a closed heart. So, **LEADers lead heart first**. You will not LEAD effectively if you do not have God's heart, and His heart is for people, *But when He saw the multitude, He was moved with compassion on them, because they fainted, and were scattered abroad, as sheep having no shepherd* (Matthew 9:36). Even on the Cross, Jesus displays the heart of a LEADer by saying, *Father forgive them, for they know not what the do* (Luke 23:34). He was demonstrating leadership by being out in front of the people. **A LEADer will never be able to stand strong and effectively out front if they don't have a heart of love**. *When David saw the angel, he said to the Lord, "I am the one who has sinned and done wrong! But these people are as innocent as sheep - what have they done? Let your anger fall against me and my family"* (II Samuel 24:17 NLT). LEADers have to be able to take the hit from the people and, oftentimes, on behalf of the people. When the people rejected not entering the promised land that God prepared, it angered God. And right when they are about to be judged for their rebellion, the LEADer Moses steps in between God and the people as an intercessor. *I will disown them and destroy them with a plague. Then I will make you into a nation greater and mightier than they are!"* [13] *But Moses objected. "What will the Egyptians think when they hear about it?" he asked the Lord. "They know full well the power you displayed in rescuing your people from Egypt.* [19] *In keeping with your magnificent, unfailing love, please* *pardon the sins of this people, just as you have forgiven them ever since they left Egypt." 20 Then the Lord said, "I will pardon them **as you have requested*** (Numbers 14:12-13; 19-20 NLT). What a clear demonstration of a LEADer's love for God's people.

LEADing is not always easy. When you said yes to LEAD, you agreed to lay down your life. Your body is no longer under your governing; it is now the property of Holy Spirit. This means that as a LEADer, your purpose is to govern your affairs and treat others as God would have you and not as you believe the person deserves. Just imagine if God chose to operate on conditional love. Love never considers the person; **it is a function of the Spirit apart from the condition of man**. It is also how God responds to us in spite of our own shortcomings. Love requires that you have and maintain a spiritual toughness of skin, and nothing is taken personally, *If the world hate you, ye know that it hated me before it hated you. 19 If ye were of the world, the world would love his own: but because ye are not of the world, but I have chosen you out of the world, therefore the world hateth you. 20 Remember the word that I said unto you, The servant is not greater than his lord. If they have persecuted me, they will also persecute you; if they have kept my saying, they will keep yours also. 21 But all these things will they do unto you for my name's sake, because they know not him that sent me* (John 15:18-21).

From God - To Us - Through Us - To Others

The one way I protect my heart is to give from my heart because if I'm giving from my heart, I'm giving from God in me. The problem arises when we do things around or apart from God out of feeling-based love. We let our feelings and emotions guide our decisions. We leave ourselves unprotected because there is no breastplate of righteousness to shield us from the faults of others. The order of our relationship with people starts with our relationship with God. It should be = **FROM GOD - TO US - THROUGH US - TO OTHERS**. Notice that the start is with God, and the follow-through is with God. So, when dealing with people, you are dealing with people through God. This is so important as a LEADer. We have to learn how to get "us" out of the way and allow the God in us to deal with His people.

It would be easy to LEAD without loving if the assignment involved more than just giving information. LEADers are building something within people, and this causes us to have to deal with the good, the bad, and the ugly. But love deepens the LEADer's devotion and commitment. If the love component is absent, the God factor is missing, and it is with love and kindness that God draws all men. It was because of His love that He gave His Son to save the world (John 3:6). It was love that caused Jesus to lay down His life, and the LEADer must possess that same love and that same laying down of his life (Galatians 2:20).

Love is so crucial because it covers many sins (missteps, hang-ups, and faults). And because people are at the center of God's heart and gifts are in earthen vessels, people are at different stages of growth and development. And until spiritual maturity is a lifestyle habit, they are bound to do, say, treat people wrong and carry out ungodly actions. This is where Godly love steps in. *Love never gives up. Love is very patient and kind, never jealous or envious, never boastful or proud, ⁵ never haughty or selfish or rude. Love does not demand its own way. It is not irritable or touchy. It does not hold grudges and will hardly even notice when others do it wrong. ⁶ It is never glad about injustice, but rejoices whenever truth wins out. ⁷ If you love someone, you will be loyal to him no matter what the cost. You will always believe in him, always expect the best of him, and always stand your ground in defending him* (I Corinthians 13:4-7 TLB).

It would be safe to say that most LEADers do a decent job at teaching the Word, but it is this action of love that most LEADers do a poor job demonstrating. Too often in the body of Christ, you hear of LEADers operating out of character or reciprocating the actions that were done to them. God's pulpit, which should be used to grow the saint, is often used as a place to get someone straight, when at that moment, what should be seen is the greatest demonstration of love. It is not a subject that we just teach to the people; more importantly, it is a life action that we must demonstrate and live out because the LEADer is given to the people by God as a part of His heart. **The LEADer to the people is the love of God.**

Someone once said that LEADing is like being a police officer; you only get one shot. LEADers who lack the fruit of love are a danger to the body of Christ. **Think of all the things that God could have used to draw the sinner and grow the saint, and the three principle things are His love, kindness, and His goodness.**

LEADing deals directly with a person's true nature, the raw material of their lives. So, you need love so that the carnal nature of people does not taint you as Holy Spirit is processing them, and you are able to look past all of that and see the potential. This is why a LEADer has to develop the characteristic of seeing people through the eyes of God. The eyes of God look through the lens of love. *The LORD hath appeared of old unto me, saying, Yea, I have loved thee with an everlasting love: therefore with lovingkindness have I drawn thee* (Jeremiah 31:3). Nothing can be taken personal, *But all these things will they do unto you for My Name's sake, because they know not Him that sent Me* (John 15:21). In addition, the LEADer also must intentionally deepen themselves in the fruit of the Spirit (Galatian 5:2-23).

God requiring a LEADer to love should not be a hard thing, and I'll explain why. It's because **God does not require the LEADer to love from them; He's simply tasking the LEADer to love with Him**. This becomes difficult only when the LEADer presumes ownership of that love. **Agape love does not belong to us; therefore, we cannot measure how much we give or if we should give it because it has been freely given to all**

of us. Agape is unconditional, and it behoves the LEADer not to delegate love under conditions but to allow the love that comes from God to pass through them to others, *for God so loved the world that He gave ...* (John 3:16).

Will people misuse and abuse the LEADers? Absolutely! Does the LEADer often get mistreated and the short end of the stick? You bet they do! Does it seem like they get off, and the LEADer is often left with the hurt and repercussions? Oh my! But not one LEADer had to die for them. The LEADer only has to die to themselves. It comes with the assignment. God keeps good books. And there is no reward for retaliation but a blessing for obedience, *and being found in fashion as a man, He humbled Himself, and became obedient unto death, even the death of the cross. 9 Wherefore God also hath highly exalted Him, and given Him a name which is above every name* (Philippians 2:8-9). At the moment, it seems like you are on the losing end, but like Jesus, you have to look past the Cross you are required to carry in the moment and see the reward of the seat. Love is not excusing the other person's actions, but as Dr. Michael Moore says, "God does not hold us responsible for what people do to us, but God holds us 100% accountable to how we adequately respond and how we adequately resolve."

LEADer, your protection against a hardened heart and the delay of blessing is the love of God. It shields our hearts from becoming tainted. It settles our emotions and keeps us bathed in the grace of God. The love of God also proves whose child you are, *But I say unto you, Love* *your enemies, bless them that curse you, do good to them that hate you, and pray for them which despitefully use you, and persecute you;* **45** **that ye may be the children of your Father which is in heaven:** *for He maketh his sun to rise on the evil and on the good, and sendeth rain on the just and on the unjust.* **46** *For if ye love them which love you, what reward have ye? do not even the publicans the same?* **47** *And if ye salute your brethren only, what do ye more than others? do not even the publicans so?* **48** *Be ye therefore perfect, even as your Father which is in heaven is perfect* (Matthew 5:45-48). I hear people always say that nobody is perfect, but according to the scripture, Biblical perfection is in how you treat others and not in not sinning. And this perfection is attainable by every believer and should be sought out with the utmost urgency in the life of the LEADer.

> An unloving LEADer will miss loving moments and corrupt LEADing.

The key to maintaining a heart of love is developing a love for righteousness. Peter was so ready to follow Jesus wherever He went, but when his heart was tested against his words, that same motive wasn't there. In the moment, He actually denied Jesus, but Jesus did not leave Peter there. He approached Peter again and asked him three times if he loved Him. And then Jesus tells Peter to "feed My Sheep." I hope that the LEADer sees from this story that Jesus requires Peter to give to or feed His sheep with love. Peter denied Jesus with a responsive reaction. This is when an unfavourable moment causes one to back out of their word or commitment. But love pushes through disparagement to reach a greater reward - Jesus calls them His sheep. And though they will sometimes act and respond as goats and butt everything, the responsive view of love is that they are His sheep, that He died for.

| Chapter 12

Discipline

I don't know about you, but I'm running hard for the
finish line. I'm giving it everything I've got. No lazy living
for me! I'm staying alert and in top condition. I'm not
going to get caught napping, telling everyone else all
about it and then missing out myself.
I Corinthians 9:26-27 MSG

You have a course to finish! Everything you've read so far
and will read is about accomplishing your assignment's
success. Every assignment from God is marked with
success, but the manifestation of that success is tied to
the LEADer's discipline. Discipline is simply *enforced
obedience*. Although, as LEADers, we come outfitted with
assignments, we must build in us the moral character
and discipline necessary to fulfil those assignments.
What Satan is really after is the sabotage of your
assignment. His overall objective is to distract the

LEADer and get them off course because if the LEADer is off course, those with whom God has connected to their course are also affected. I don't think LEADers really understand that it's much bigger than just them. I think most LEADers only see it as their call, assignment, and purpose, and if they don't finish or mess up, it only affects them. But this is so far from the truth and plays directly into the hands of Satan. Being a LEADer has to do with so much more than just you. The word alone suggests that there are followers, and your outcome impacts the follower(s). Jesus died on the Cross, but it was for the world. His assignment involved the world. His getting out of the ground had the future condition of humanity at stake (John 3:16-17, Ephesians 2:1, Colossians 1:12-13, Hebrews 2:10).

There is something that God has put in you to complete and finish on earth, and things are at stake to your completion. What will be squandered, stuck, or have to defer to the next arising LEADer because you did not attain the discipline to complete the course given to you? This is why discipline is so important. There is a level of obedience and personal accountability that you have to enforce on your own self. Sometimes our callings and giftings can become our archenemy. By that, I mean that we can become so in-tune with the ebb and flows of gifting, talent, and anointing that we disregard and overlook the disciplining of ourselves that provides check and balance in our character, integrity, and personal devotion to God, *that ye **put off concerning the former conversation the old man**, which is corrupt* *according to the deceitful lusts;* [24] *and that ye* **put on the new man***, which after God is created in righteousness and true holiness* (Ephesians 4:22,24). **When there is no discipline of putting off and putting on, LEADers are gifted-strong but morally imbalanced.** LEADers become deceived into thinking that gifts, talent, and anointing relieve the duty of disciplining one's life and correcting one's errors. Satan will back up and allow you to do your best work. One of his greatest traps is hidden comfort. I remember one time I was preaching my greatest message after watching porn. I told myself I was still anointed and it couldn't be that bad. How could it be when God just moved like that? And then the Spirit of God said, "Yeah, God is being glorified, but you are dying inside." And He was right. I wasn't reading the Word and putting in the necessary time with God. I knew how to give my mind and body over to the work of the Lord. I knew how to get out of the way on the stage. And that safety had become my comfort. It was a false discipline because I wasn't working on myself. I was just gifted strong while morally imbalanced. **I'm not writing something that I studied.** That is the difference with this LEADership book. **Each of these Chapters are lived experiences.** And I want you to know that it's important to know where and how you are gifted - it doesn't even take much because if done correctly, you are simply giving over to God a body that He is now in use of, like Peter and his boat to Jesus. But if you are void of, or uncaring of your need of personal discipline, the boat will soon sink, *but I keep under my body, and bring it into subjection: lest that by any means,* **when I have preached** *to others, I myself should be a castaway* (I Corinthians 9:27). Yea, you may not be taking glory from God, but its just as worse to not give glory to God in your body.

Don't be deceived that the fruit of the gift, the working of the talent, and the power of the anointing are for you. That is the glory that belongs and goes to God. Eli was a prophet who raised and trained the great prophet Samuel. But his lack of discipline brought him and his sons to doom. Even the ark of God [the presence of God] was taken away (I Samuel 412-18). This story of Eli and his sons is very important because it shows what often becomes the result of LEAders that are gift strong and have no discipline. I would suggest that you read I Samuel 2:27-29 and see the potential of what can happen to those who work for the Lord but lack personal discipline in their lives. Are not LEAders dying the same way? There is no new thing under the sun. This Bible was given to us as an example, so we can see ahead and avoid the same outcome from happening in our lives (I Timothy 4:15-16, II Timothy 3:16-17).

There are four key areas that LEADer must be attentive in disciplining themselves in.

1. Your Infirmity - An infirmity is simply a bend in your flesh. We all have something in our flesh that we are bent towards. You must know what that is and put boundaries and safeguards around you and between it, *For I know that in me (that is, in my flesh)* **dwelleth no good thing** (Romans 7:18a).

Transparency - My infirmity was pornography, which falls under the category of the lust of the flesh, *For all that is in the world - the lust of the flesh [craving for sensual gratification] and the lust of the eyes [greedy longings of the mind] and the pride of life [assurance in one's own resources or in the stability of earthly things] - these do not come from the Father but are from the world [itself]* (I John 2:16AMPC). My **safeguard** *(plural)* was my wife knowing. An open phone that my wife, kids, and staff had open access to. An accountability partner other than my wife that I could call, pray with, and who would be praying for me. I went back to find its root cause and prayed against it. I also learned not to put certain things before my eyes that would trigger the emotion. And I learned at what times Satan or my flesh would rise up in that area. I received that God has forgiven all my iniquities so that if I fell short, I would not fall into condemnation. I pray in the Spirit, and lean heavily on the help and aid of Holy Spirit.

2. The Balance of Life - Many LEADers have sacrificed marriages, family, and mental and physical health for ministry. And sadly, they do it all in the Name of Christ Jesus. The truth is that their lives and homes are in disarray because they gave no balance to it. *The blessing of the Lord - it makes [truly] rich, and He adds no sorrow with it [neither does toiling increase it* (Proverbs 10:22 AMPC). How is Christ the center of it, and it's all in disarray? It conflicts with the message the LEADer carries. It is also confusing when LEADers can preach a Gospel to others that should bring order to their lives, and it is not lived out in the life of the one who LEADs with it, *That ye be not slothful, but followers of them who through faith and patience inherit the promises* (Hebrews 6:12). *Ye are the light of the world. A city that is set on an hill cannot be hid. 15 Neither do men light a candle, and put it under a bushel, but on a candlestick; and it giveth light unto all that are in the house* (Matthew 5:14-15). LEADers should at some point, if not already, have the proof of what they teach, *So then, **by their fruit,** you will recognize them* (Matthew 7:20 NLT). There should be balance in the LEADers' life - nothing missing, nothing broken. But LEADers often experince the unintended consequences of a life that has no balance, *Put first things first* (Proverbs 24:27aAMPC).

This also deals with the LEADer being able to say no: *Let your Yes be simply Yes, and your No be simply No: anything more than that comes from the evil one* (Matthew 5:37 AMPC). No isn't a bad word. It is a repellent to imbalance and an incompetent yes. God did not call us to be everything for everybody or to do everything for everybody. **The LEADer must learn how to stay in their lane and know when something is beyond their ability to do**.

3. Time with God - Time with God includes the LEADer's prayer and meditation, Bible study, message prep, personal spiritual growth, etc. These are the tools in the tool belt of the Kingdom LEADer. Kingdom LEADers should be diligent in becoming skilled in using their tools, as well as being sharpened for use, *Study and be* *eager and do your utmost to present yourself to God approved (tested by trial), a workman who has no cause to be ashamed, correctly analyzing and accurately dividing [rightly handling and skillfully teaching] the Word of Truth* (II Timothy 2:15 AMPC). Unfortunately, many who are called do not continue in the necessity of things that the call needs. There are LEADers who only go into times of prayer, reading, and studying when it is time to do the work. This is a performance-based relationship; eventually, the messages will tell the truth. These moments are just as important to who the LEADer is as they are to what the LEADer does. But if they only see them necessary for doing and not being, eventually they will lose in the doing also, *Therefore we ought to give the more earnest heed to the things which we have heard, lest at any time we should let them slip* (Hebrews 2:1).

4. Personal Growth and Maturity - No LEADer should remain a novice. LEADers should be disciplined towards personal growth. *These things command and teach. 12 Let no man despise thy youth; but be thou an example of the believers, in word, in conversation, in charity, in spirit, in faith, in purity. 13 Till I come, give attendance to reading, to exhortation, to doctrine. 14 Neglect not the gift that is in thee, which was given thee by prophecy, with the laying on of the hands of the presbytery. 15 Meditate upon these things; give thyself wholly to them; that thy profiting may appear to all. 16 Take heed unto thyself, and unto the doctrine; continue in them: for in doing this thou shalt both save thyself, and them that hear thee* (I Timothy 4:11-16). In the same way, we are LEADing others to grow in God, and it is imperative that the LEADer is operating in a discipline that causes them to grow in their own lives.

| Chapter 13

A Commitment to Excellence

LEADer Note:
Be disciplined enough to stay true
to your assignment.

Jesus commanded them not to tell anyone. But the more
he did so, the more they kept talking about it. **37** People
were overwhelmed with amazement.
"He has done everything well."
Mark 7:36-37 NIV

Daniel

The Bible tells us why Daniel was elevated above 120
men. *Then this <u>Daniel was preferred above the presidents</u>
<u>and princes,</u> **because an excellent spirit was in him;** *and*
the king thought to set him over the whole realm (Daniel
6:3). We know that Daniel was a pinpoint prophet, but
Daniel's elevation happened because he had an excellent
spirit. It was not until they could find no fault against
Daniel and the kingdom (his duty of operation) that they
tried to find an occasion against him and God. *Then the*
presidents and princes sought to find occasion against

Daniel concerning the kingdom; but they could find none occasion nor fault; forasmuch as he was faithful, neither was there any error or fault found in him. ⁵ Then said these men, We shall not find any occasion against this Daniel, except we find it against him concerning the law of his God (Daniel 6:4-5).

From Daniel

Daniel's service to God did not exclude him from being a man of excellence; because of that, he was preferred over 120 men. Daniel shows us that we are not only responsible for the care of the gifts but also for how we function apart from them. Daniel's secular life was not dissimilar to his spiritual walk, meaning you did not find him outside of excellence no matter what he did. Excellence is a part of his makeup. How ironic is it that the first thing they tried to find was a fault in his natural abilities, and they could not.

A Commitment to Excellence

As a Kingdom LEADer, what you do and how you do it is important. You are representing the Creator of all things. The presentation of yourself, the Word, your service, and whatever moves through your hands speaks of and to the One you are doing it for. Therefore, it must always be the best. I believe that God deserves the best this world has to offer, at whatever level you are at. If God gave man the wisdom to invent it, then God should have it. We shouldn't want to give God any less than what He gave us. He gave His only begotten Son. It was the best seed God could offer.

It is saddening to see LEADers who do not prepare themselves and who do not place a high value on the Word. There is this demonic statement that the Church has accepted, and it has even bled over into how we serve God. That statement says, "It does not take all that." The ironic thing is that only the Church has accepted that. The world doesn't accept mediocre. We look for the best hotels. We don't accept anything from the restaurant kitchen or eat at them if they are dirty. No, we put our bodies in the best we can afford, yet give anything to God when He deserves the best. Shouldn't the One that made it have the best of it? I wonder if anyone asked God if it took all that when we read about how He utfitted Heaven?

When I hear that statement or something similar to it, it is obvious that the person has not read God's direction to Moses on how He wanted His sanctuary to be built (Exodus 25). Everything wood was to be overlayed in gold. The curtain hooks were made of silver and gold. The oils were imported and mixed with other precious ointments. Candlesticks of pure gold. Curtains of fine-wined linen. Even the priest's garments were tailored to God's liking with precious stones made in them. (Read Exodus Chapter 25-28.) God is excellent and extravagant, but not wasteful.

This same excellence is what convinced the Queen of Sheba that she could inquire of King Solomon of all that was in her heart, *And when the queen of Sheba had **seen all Solomon's wisdom**, and the house that he had built, 5 and the meat of his table, and the sitting of his servants, and the attendance of his ministers, and their apparel, and his cupbearers, **and his ascent by which he went up unto the house of the Lord**; there was no more spirit in her. 6 And she said to the king, It was a true report that I heard in mine own land of thy acts and of thy wisdom. 7 Howbeit I believed not the words, until I came, and mine eyes had seen it: and, behold, the half was not told me: thy wisdom and prosperity exceedeth the fame which I heard. 8 Happy are thy men, happy are these thy servants, which stand continually before thee, and that hear thy wisdom* (I Kings 10:4-8).

It mattered to the men of old how they presented and represented God, *But King David answered Araunah, "No, I will pay the full price for the land. I won't take anything that is yours and give it to the LORD. **I won't offer a burnt offering that costs me nothing**"* (I Chronicles 21:24 NCV). *Then Pharaoh sent and called Joseph, and they brought him hastily out of the dungeon: and **he shaved himself, and changed his raiment**, and came in unto Pharaoh* (Genesis 41:14). *And it came to pass, <u>when the king sat in his house</u>, and the Lord had given him rest round about from all his enemies; 2 that the king said unto Nathan the prophet, See now, <u>I dwell in an house of cedar</u>, **but the ark of God dwelleth within curtains**. 3 And Nathan said to the king, Go, **do all that is in thine heart**;*

for the Lord is with thee (II Samuel 7:1-3). Excellence isn't new; it has just gone overlooked and thought to be unneeded. If we look back at the Queen of Sheba, she said that <u>she saw Solomon's wisdom</u>. Now she came with the question to hear Solomon's wisdom but knew she'd get her answer from seeing what his wisdom had produced. **EVERYTHING WE DO, WE SHOULD DO IT WITH EXCELLENCE**! For God, we should have a desire to go beyond good. Because we are called, it is easy to put a message together. Preaching is actually the easiest thing you will do. But when you take the time to factor in excellence, you can't just serve God's people anything because it is seen as what God wanted them to have. And God never gives less than the best.

In the opening scripture, it says that the people kept talking about Jesus. And the talk was about how well He did everything. In church circles, we talk a lot about miracles, signs, and wonders. We are thirsting for gifts - and we absolutely should be. But have we ever stopped to think that those signs and wonders are associated with the deliverance of excellence? Or are we even concerned about how it looks or focused on the things that speak but have no voice?

Be excellent! Excellence is doing your best, giving your best, and being your best in all things. It is akin to integrity - even when it might not be seen, it's still maintained in excellence because God sees all. And He who sees you in private will reward you openly.

I am convinced that many have yet to see the fullness of what they are capable of producing because God will not allow them to bring shame upon His Name. *Then this Daniel was preferred above the presidents and princes, **because an excellent spirit was in him**; and the king thought to set him over the whole realm (Daniel 6:3).* We are talking about a king that did not serve Jehovah God, but wanted one of His servants as LEAD. Even in his palace, there were certain specifications required in choosing who would serve. Anything wouldn't do, *And the king spake unto Ashpenaz the master of his eunuchs, that he should **bring certain of the children of Israel**, and of the king's seed, and of the princes; 4 children in whom was no blemish, but well favoured, and skilful in all wisdom, and cunning in knowledge, and understanding science, and such as had ability in them to stand in the king's palace, and whom they might teach the learning and the tongue of the Chaldeans* (Daniel 1:3-4).

There have been many of God's children who have lost what they had and where they were positioned simply because they didn't realise that it was that extra that got them there. Truthfully speaking, you are held to a higher standard the higher you go. But people are less likely to hold you to a level of accountability because of where you are. So, it takes personal obligation that says **I will only and always give my best or nothing at all**. Personally speaking, it saddens me to see a pastor or LEADer standing before the people looking like they just got off the couch. They either don't understand that they represent God or don't care much. Some will want to go spiritual and say, "*man looketh on the outer appearance, but God looks at the heart.*" My reply would be, "*Well, look at the cook and not at the nasty kitchen and dirty plate.*" The problem is that we've become accustomed to not caring what we give God, while at the same time, we want nothing less than exceptional from ourselves, "*When you say, 'The altar of GOD is not important anymore; worship of GOD is no longer a priority,' that's defiling. And when you offer worthless animals for sacrifices in worship, animals that you're trying to get rid of - blind and sick and crippled animals -isn't that defiling? Try a trick like that with your banker or your senator - how far do you think it will get you?" GOD-of-the-Angel-Armies asks you. "Get on your knees and pray that I will be gracious to you. You priests have gotten everyone in trouble. With this kind of conduct, do you think I'll pay attention to you?" GOD-of-the-Angel-Armies asks you* (Malachi 1:7-9 MSG).

Be excellent! Give God your best. We should want all that we do for God to be accepted by Him. You signed on with your "Yes, Lord," which was an agreement to give the best in everything you do. When royalty shows up, everyone expects to see the finest. Well, you are a royal priesthood, a son and daughter of the King, chosen to function in His Kingdom as an ambassador. What you have been tasked to carry is precious and valuable. It was God who commanded that everything made of wood in His house be covered with gold. Wood represented humanity, and gold represented pureness. This was done so that the people would see and receive the best. You say that's the Old Testament. Yes, it is! And if we follow the progressive revelation of the Bible into the New Testament, you and I are covered - actually, we're hidden in Christ. So, that same covering of old so that God is seen still covers us today so that Christ is revealed.

| Chapter 14

Obedience

And why call ye Me, 'Lord, Lord,' and do not
the things which I say?
Luke 6:46

There is a story about a young prophet from Judah who was sent to prophesy to Jeroboam. He was also charged by the Word of the Lord to *eat no bread, drink water, or turn again by the same way that thou camest.* In the same city was an old prophet who got word and sent his son to find the young prophet. When the young prophet was found, he was asked to come home and eat bread. The young prophet then rehearsed what the Lord had charged him with, and that was *to say, the lord said to me by the word of the Lord, Thou shalt eat no bread nor drink water there, nor turn again to go by the way that thou camest* (I Kings 13). But the old prophet replied that he was a prophet as thou art; *an angel spake unto me by the word of the Lord, saying, Bring him back with thee into thine house, that he may eat bread and drink water.* But he lied unto him. So the young prophet returned with him, ate bread in his house, and drank water. While eating, the old prophet who actually lied prophesies the truth and says, *Thus saith the Lord, Forasmuch as thou hast disobeyed the mouth of the Lord, and hast not kept the commandment which the Lord thy God commanded thee, ²² but camest back, and hast eaten bread and drunk water in the place, <u>of the which the Lord did say to thee</u>,* **Eat no bread, and drink no water; thy carcase shall not come unto the sepulchre of thy fathers** (I Kings 13:21-22). The young prophet ate the meal, left, and died in the way just as the Lord said. Here is what was said of the young prophet and not the old, *It is the man of God,* **who was disobedient unto the word of the Lord**: *therefore the Lord hath delivered him unto the lion, which hath torn him, and slain him, according to the word of the Lord, which he spake unto him (v.26).*

Disobedience cost! In the aforementioned story, the young prophet's disobedience cost him his life and his kingdom career. The shocking thing is that the story does not reveal to us if anything happened to the old prophet for lying and persuading the young prophet. I believe this is because the focus was never on what others would say, but on the young prophet's commitment of obedience to God. Is it possible that God was not using the older prophet in this season of his life for the same reason? Which is why the young prophet was called from far when there was one near? The point is that we may never see the result of a loss of life from our disobedience, but how many potential LEADers are not being used by God because of disobedience on their part? *If ye be willing and obedient, ye shall eat the good of the land: 20 But if ye refuse and rebel, ye shall be devoured with the sword: for the mouth of the Lord hath spoken it* (Isaiah 1:19-20). Again, the focus is solely on the obedience of the young prophet. What did God tell him to do? His actions were not just missteps or mistakes. He knew what the orders were and chose to do the opposite because someone with a likened title said otherwise. *Then Peter and the other apostles answered and said,* **We ought to obey God rather than men** (Acts 5:29).

At the end of the day, **LEADers are fully accountable to God**, not men. It did not matter that the old prophet lied; what mattered was what the young prophet was told. **Pinpointing the blame will never work when you disobey an order God has given you**. It does not matter what others are doing. They may seem to be getting by doing things their way or without God's consent. God will not hold one LEADer accountable or charge a LEADer for the erroneous actions of another. **Are you in obedience to what God has told you?** Maybe that's why the Bible identified the one prophet in the town as old, but now the young prophet is dead. Don't allow disobedience to cause you to die [be separated] from your God-given instructions or die [become separated] from being used by God, *And being found in fashion as a man, he humbled himself, and became obedient unto death, even the death of the cross. 8And being found in human form,* <u>He humbled</u>

147

Himself **by becoming obedient to the point of death,** *even death on a Cross* - Philippians 2:7-8.

LEADers have to have this bold confidence to obey God even when others don't understand, disagree, or can't see what you see. They weren't there when God said it or showed it to you. And if it were that important that they see, agree, and understand, then God would have called a meeting and told all at the same time. You have to have a resolute mind to obey God no matter the cost. As a LEADers, you have to be willing to stand alone and obey if needed. **Better alone in obedience than with many in disobedience**. Peter, the closest of the Apostles to Jesus heard, *"Satan, the Lord rebuke you,"* for trying to stop Jesus from getting to the Cross, while Judas was called a friend because He was not hindering Him from being obedient in getting to the Cross (Matthew 16:23).

It's not perfect LEADers God is looking for; it's obedient LEADers. The gift is in earthen vessels, so perfection is the aim, but it's not the goal. Furthermore, perfection from a Biblical perspective is not about always getting it right and not making any mistakes (Ecclesiastes 7:20). We learned in a previous Chapter that Biblical perfection deals with our treatment and response to others (Matthew 5:43-48). None of the men Jesus used was perfect. But all were required to be obedient. You will make mistakes along your LEADership journey, but disobedience is one mistake you must stay free of.

- Adam and Eve disobeyed God and introduced sin into the world and humanity.

- Saul was fired and served in the seat as king of Israel for 20 years and didn't know. He disobeyed God and didn't do as the Lord said.

- Gehazi should have been Elisha's successor, but he disobeyed Elisha and, behind his back, asked for what Elisha said not to take. He lost his position and was cursed with leprosy.

- Abraham and Sarah disobeyed God and tried to create a promise that God said He would give through their loins. They birthed an Ishmael, and the siblings' rivalry is still present today.

- When the children of Israel disobeyed God, they fell into the hands of their enemies, got sick, lost wars, and generations died off.

- Moses disobeyed God and smote the rock instead of speaking to it as God said, and lost out on him LEADing the children of Israel into Canaan.

These are just a few accounts of the outcomes of LEADers and people that disobeyed God. What LEADers must keep in mind is that the response to **the call of LEADership is not as you want - it's as you are led**. And the response to being led is obedience, *Know ye not, that to whom ye yield yourselves servants to obey, his servants ye are to whom ye obey; whether of sin unto death, or of obedience unto righteousness* (Romans 6:16).

| Chapter 15

Walk Forgiving

And when ye stand praying, forgive, if ye have ought against any: that your Father also which is in heaven may forgive you your trespasses. [26] But if ye do not forgive, neither will your Father which is in heaven forgive your trespasses.

Mark 11:25-26

My father in the faith, Dr. Michael Moore Sr., founder and former pastor of Faith Chapel Christian Center, Birmingham, Alabama, taught me something very important about dealing with God's people. One of the things he taught was that the LEADer was not responsible for people. That it is possible to be responsible for people and miss God. He said that a LEADer's responsibility was to God, and by virtue of being responsible to God, they would automatically be responsible to people. That lesson alone changed everything for me. I could see how easy it would be to be led by people's desires and wants and totally miss God's leading.

The second thing he taught me about people is that **God does not hold LEADers responsible for what people do to them, but God holds the LEADer one hundred percent responsible for how they adequately resolve and adequately respond**. This was big! From this lesson, I saw how LEADers hold on to hurt, which turns into disdain towards people and a dislike towards the ministry. It happens because they don't respond to wrongs properly and quickly. Let's look at Colossians 3:13 in a few translations:

KJV - *forbearing one another, **and forgiving one another**, if any man have a quarrel against any: even as Christ forgave you, so also do ye.*

TLB - ***Be gentle and ready to forgive; never hold grudges**. Remember, the Lord forgave you, so you must forgive others.*

NLT - ***Make allowance for each other's faults**, and **forgive anyone who offends you**. Remember, the Lord forgave you, so you must forgive others.*

MSG - ***Be even-tempered, content with second place**, and **quick to forgive an offense. Forgive as quickly and completely** as the Master forgave you. And regardless of what else you put on, wear love. It's your basic, all-purpose garment. Never be without it.*

Because LEADers are in the people business, to walk forgiving is a very important attribute. I tell the members of my Church that as a pastor, I deal with a part of people that they would possibly never see or engage. Even their closest friends and relatives won't. Sometimes even spouses, because as a pastor, I am dealing directly with the person's spiritual nature. You may say your friend would never do that, but as a LEADer, I understand that you may never engage that side of them. The storm that met Jesus when crossing over was caused by a spirit in the man that the people were binding with chains and fetters but to no avail (Mark Chapter 5). When Jesus made it over, He engaged the spirit inside, whose name was Legion, and many others. In Matthew 16:23, Peter rebukes Jesus, but Jesus turns to Peter and addresses Satan. *But he turned, and said unto Peter, Get thee behind me, Satan: thou art an offence unto me: for thou savourest not the things that be of God, but those that be of men.* It is important that the LEADer understands this because we deal with the authentic nature of people - their spirit man. And it is possible that the person doesn't even realize that they are dealing with a spiritual matter.

Offense Free

LEADers must be conscious of staying offense free so that they can freely give of the Spirit and not become tainted victims of people's actions. There will be people who do things intentionally and unintentionally. Either way, both must be forgiven. Because many LEADers do not walk forgiving, they are LEADing with broken spirits and harbored offense in their hearts. This eventually comes out in their message and their LEADing. What's even more dangerous is if they are over a group of people, that harbored offense spills over into their lives as well. This is why the Bible says, *be quick to forgive*, because the LEADer can't carry spillage and think that it is okay because it only stays with them. LEADers don't carry cares, they cast cares.

Unforgiveness is poison. Its roots are very strong, and they go deep into the heart. They choke out love, trust, empathy, and compassion. That's why several of those translations aforementioned said to <u>forgive quickly</u> so that there is no space for growth, and you kill off the root of bitterness and becoming resentful. It does damage to a LEADer and everything connected to them. EVERY LEADer will be faced with the opportunity to become offended. Did you hear what I just said? It's an opportunity to be offended. Someone, at some point in life, is going to do something offensive; intentionally or unintentionally, and at that moment, you have the choice to be offended. And if you remain offended, it is because you choose to be. Proverbs 28:14YLT says, *O the happiness of a man fearing continually, And **whoso is hardening his heart falleth into evil**.* Notice in the scripture that the heart was hardened by the person possessing the heart and not the wrong that came to them. When you do not forgive, you are choosing to harden your heart, and the result of a hardened heart is a broken spirit. *The strong spirit of a man sustains him in bodily pain or trouble, but a weak and broken spirit who can raise up or bear?* (Proverbs 18:14 AMPC). **Walk forgiving is the shield that keeps the contamination**

of offence from getting in. You have to choose not to be offended and choose to forgive quickly. I love John 14:1a: *let not your heart be troubled.* Every LEADer should paste this scripture on their forehead of their heart. I say that because trouble is coming. We are dealing with people; some are immature, hurt, broken, need guidance, and just plain evil, and you have you to choose to not let your heart be troubled. At the Cross, Jesus had an opportunity to be offended and not forgive. It would seem fair not to because He had done no wrong, which is the trick of unforgiveness. To make you believe that you have the right to hold offense. But holding offense does nothing to the other person, only to the heart of the one offended. So, like Jesus, we must too must confess, *Father forgive them for they know not what they do* (Luke 23:34).

Knowing this, **the LEADer must prepare themselves to take nothing personally**. Accept that it comes with the assignment so that they come away unscathed by the actions of others. Remember, Jesus said you would be persecuted for righteous sake (Matthew 5:10). John 15:10 says, *Remember the word that I said unto you, The servant is no greater than his Lord. **If they have persecuted Me, they will also persecute you**; if they have kept My saying, they will keep yours also.* And the anthem for every LEADer is Second Corinthians 4:7-12, *But we have this treasure in earthen vessels, that the excellency of the power may be of God, and not of us. 8 We are troubled on every side, yet not distressed; we are perplexed, but not in despair; 9 persecuted, but not forsaken; cast down, but not destroyed; 10 always bearing* *about in the body the dying of the Lord Jesus, that the life also of Jesus might be made manifest in our body. ¹¹ **For we which live are always delivered unto death for Jesus' sake**, that the life also of Jesus might be made manifest in our mortal flesh. ¹² So then death worketh in us, but life in you.*

Walk forgiving! It keeps you off the hook of heartbreak. You cannot walk as an effective LEADer with pessimism in your heart towards people. **No one deserves to be served the iniquity in you that you chose to carry from not forgiving someone else**. If there is unforgiveness in your heart, let it go today and allow Holy Spirit to fill your heart with God's love. Serve forward from a heart filled with the love of God.

| Chapter 16
BEWARE!

Leader Note:
You are checking on everyone else, who are you checking in with?

For I know that in me (that is, in my flesh,) dwelleth no good thing: for to will is present with me; but how to perform that which is good I find not.
Romans 7:18

The front has its challenges. All eyes are on you. There is this inclination to always present oneself at your best. LEADers cannot put their sorrows before the people. LEADers can't put their life challenges before the people; they are coming to us for answers to their challenges. What that often suggests to the people is that LEADers have it all together and have no problems. And although this is the furthest from the truth and unfair, it comes with the position. We can tell them that we are imperfect and have flaws, but that doesn't change the fact of how they see LEADers in their eyes.

But here lies the problem: LEADers know **they are imperfect and have flaws. They have no one to whom they purposefully hold themselves accountable to**. So, the LEADer ignores the same principle of partnering accountability they teach. **Two are better than one is not only good for the taught, but also for the teacher**. Too many LEADers are found to fall when they do not have to. LEADers have accepted and embraced their fleshly desires and have fallen into the sifting trap of Satan. **You aren't good just because no one knows; it is unseen**. You are actually in danger of collapse. The scripture says that we are to *confess our faults one to another, and pray one for another, that ye may be healed. The effectual fervent prayer of a righteous man availeth much* - James 5:16. What Satan does is he makes having the title LEADer and the front give you a sense of invincibility while setting a trap for your demise.

Who Is Watching Out For You?

Have you shared with anyone your proclivities and weaknesses? Who are you checking in with, and can you be totally transparent and naked in front of them? What's your Achilles heel? We all have a no good thing, *For I know that in me (that is, in my flesh) dwelleth no good thing.*

I believe that there was a reason why Jesus sent the disciples out two by two. I never go to speak alone. Not that I have intentions of doing anything, but I put no trust in my flesh. I never make the assumption that "I'm a

LEADer, and I would never." Though that is my aim, I am also aware that I have an adversary whose mission in life is to take me out, and I deliberately close as many loopholes as possible to destroy the enemy's plot. King David should have been on the battlefield, but he was at home on the rooftop, where he knew Bathsheba was. He then enquired about her and waited until her time as a minstrel was over to lie with her. King David was in the wrong place. People get totally naked (in heart, mind, and emotion) in front of LEADers all the time, which is why LEADers must be even more cautious about keeping themselves covered and accountable.

You are anointed and chosen by God, but you are not invincible. You are housed in the flesh, and that flesh is sold under sin - it wants to act up in something(s). This does not make you an evil person, but it should definitely make you cautious. That flesh has weaknesses and vulnerabilities, and if it goes unmanaged, unmastered, and unaccountable, it will master you. **LEADer, you have to submit yourself to someone and not trust yourself to be the caretaker and watcher of you alone in this area**, *that there should be no schism in the body;* _but that the members should have the same care one for another_ (I Corinthians 12:25). Don't fall into the trap of thinking that you aren't a part of the body. That you are something special outside the body sent to give something to the body. That is decapitation. And just like with the natural body, a body part dies when it is disconnected. You too will die from delusional disconnect. There is someone you can be transparent with, which will be the best relationship you could ever have. Satan somehow uses the approval and applause of people to pump our flesh up and make us feel good. This can cause us to look over the sinful attractions, and before we know it, we are found doing something we never intended to do. The other thing Satan uses is your anointing. You will think that because you still teach effectively, lay hands, heal the sick, and testimonies are coming in from people of life change, you are doing menial work, and God is pleased. That's Satan's trap! Listen, God's Word cannot return void, and His gifts are without repentance. That's' not you; that's the gift, call, and anointing at work. You, on the other hand, are in the sifting of Satan. No sin is safe! And to think that he would use Kingdom successes to make you think that you are safe in your sins shows why he got kicked out of Heaven.

I wish LEADers wouldn't take this area so lightly. The collapse of good LEADers set the church back, and I am convinced it is because LEADers don't <u>make themselves</u> accountable to someone. Someone has to have the permission to speak constructively into your life. Here is something you must prepare for when engaging your accountability partner: extreme pushback. They will not agree with all you say. **They will challenge your intent and reason**. It will feel like they are against you. But they have your best at heart. You have to see the relationship for what it is. **They are in my life to keep me centered spiritually and free from my fleshly desires**. You will walk away mad at times. Oftentimes, LEADers get rid of these people instead of understanding their personal role in their lives and embracing them.

We do so much to prepare ourselves to be our best on stage (the front), but how well are we protecting our backs? The hidden will eventually become visible. **Darkness is to sin as light is to flowers**. Hiding doesn't cause it to die; it actually helps it to bloom. All the Chapters in this book are important, but this chapter, though short, if ignored, has lifelong consequences.

Zeal Alone

Another thing that the LEADer must beware of is zeal, which is *passion, devotion, or fire*. I am very passionate about the call of God on my life and on fire for what God has called me to do. I am not saying that we should not have zeal. Zeal isn't bad, but without the permission and partnership of Holy Spirit, zeal alone is dangerous. It puts the LEADer out in a position of operating with only their own strength and ability. Zeal alone is you in operation in the knowledge of a thing, but not in the anointing and supernatural power of the Spirit to accomplish it. This was the case with Paul. Paul knew that his call included severe persecution and even possible torment (Acts 9:16). But this did not mean that every assignment was one of such. In Acts 21, Paul was headed to Jerusalem, **but by the Spirit**, his disciples said that he should not go. Next, **a prophet named Agabus** came, and verse 11-14 says, *And when he was come unto us, he took Paul's girdle, and bound his own hands and feet, and said, **Thus saith*** *__the Holy Ghost__, So shall the Jews at Jerusalem bind the man that owneth this girdle, and shall deliver him into the hands of the Gentiles. ¹² And when we heard these things, both we, and they of that place, __besought him not to go up to Jerusalem__. ¹³ Then Paul answered, What mean ye to weep and to break mine heart? for I am ready not to be bound only, but also to die at Jerusalem for the Name of the Lord Jesus. ¹⁴ __And when he would not be persuaded, we ceased, saying, The will of the Lord be done__. The will of the Lord be done* is not implying that they were keeping from the Lord's will because of what would happen to him if he went. If that were the case, then Holy Spirit was also against God because the men and Agabus both said it was the Spirit speaking. This statement means that neither they nor Holy Spirit can usurp Paul's free will. There is much theological argument that Paul did not miss God; however, how can we deny that the Spirit gave Paul a warning three times? I am convinced that Paul missed it as a LEADer and ran with zeal. The end result was that Paul was dragged out of the city by the people, arrested, and nearly beaten to death.

__You need more than zeal__. Your passion, devotion, and fire are fueled by the Spirit of God, not assignments. It is good for LEADers to be on fire for what God wants, but we are only pre-engineered to carry out what God says.

The People's Champ

I was sitting with my pastor along with some of his spiritual sons, and I remember him saying that the problem with the Church is LEADership. They have handed the mic over to the people rather than giving them what God wants them to have. He said they play the song of what the people want, not God's words. So, our LEADers have become puppets for the people. He then turns to us, saying, "You must obey God at all costs and make of yourself no reputation."

I valued that moment. It was like Paul taking to his young spiritual son Timothy when he charged him *to preach the word; be instant in season, out of season; reprove, rebuke, exhort with all longsuffering and doctrine* (II Timothy 4:2). This was the exact same charge. To not become moved or persuaded by the people.

LEADers are not there to be a fan of the people. In the secular world, the crowd can persuade the artist of what song they want to hear, and based on the cheers, the artist will sing their song of choice. Kingdom LEADer doesn't have that option. We say what has been given to us. We are directed from above and not out from among us, *Then answered Jesus and said unto them, Verily, verily, I say unto you, The Son can do nothing of himself, but what he seeth the Father do: for what things soever he doeth, these also doeth the Son likewise* (John 5:18). King Saul wanted to be the people's champ, and it cost him the throne. The first words to the prophet Jeremiah was about not focusing on the people, *But the Lord said unto me, Say not, I am a child: **for thou shalt go to all that I shall send thee, and whatsoever I command thee thou shalt speak. 8 Be not afraid of their faces**: for I am with* *thee to deliver thee, saith the Lord.* ⁹ *Then the Lord put forth his hand, and touched my mouth. And the Lord said unto me, Behold,* **I have put my words in thy mouth** (Jeremiah 1:7-8). God's Word is in your mouth, not in the people's wants. You have to resist the urge to cater to the people and not allow the people to pedestal you. Stay humble. Give glory to God.

> The mind of Jesus was to make Himself of no reputation and that humbled Him.

The LEADer's job is to point the people to God and not to them. **You are the messenger, not the message.** Don't allow the compliments and applauses to cause you to become vain. Don't become persuaded by the current trends. Know the difference between creativity and persuasion. You carry the vision, not the people. The decisions of LEADing will not always be agreeable with people, but they should always be pleasing to God. If making people happy is your goal, you are guaranteed to have already missed God. Beware! If your focus is being the people's champ, chances are you are God's enemy.

|Chapter 17

LEADing Simplified

LEADer,

It was said earlier, but it is worth saying again that you can be as creative, savvy, unique, intelligent, and appealing as you want. And LEADers should strive to be all of these. You should want to have the full package. But having all of these culminate to being just a pretty box without the right packaging. And the packaging consists of transparency, integrity, character, and godly morals. I wanted to summarize the book with this Chapter. It is my prayer that as you are developing yourself as a top-tier LEADer, that you understand that **LEADers LEAD from within**. It was not just the body of Jesus. It was what gave life to the body that mattered also. And the aforementioned things are what give life to the quality and longevity of the LEADer you will be. The part of the stories that are most overlooked in the Bible are the ones where the LEADers self-sabotaged. I beseech you to cradle First Timothy 1:18-19, the New Living Translation, in your heart and let it guide you in your LEADership journey. *Now, Timothy, my son, here is my* *command to you: Fight well in the Lord's battles, just as the Lord told us through his prophets that you would. ¹⁹ Cling tightly to your faith in Christ and always keep your conscience clear, doing what you know is right. For some people have disobeyed their consciences and have deliberately done what they knew was wrong. It isn't surprising that soon they lost their faith in Christ after defying God like that.*

1. **Stay dependent on God**. (Acts 4:13,17:28) You cannot become gift, talent, or skill dependent. As you work to become the best LEADer, **stay dependent** on God.

2. **Your prayer life is the most important thing you have.**
   - Preparing a sermon/message is not spending time with God. MAKE VALUABLE YOUR GOD TIME!

3. **Learn to rest.** God works best in a vessel of rest. This may be one of your biggest challenges, but I am strongly convinced that it's the reason pastors are so unhealthy and have health challenges. Being under the anointing and the experiencing excitement of vision fulfilment is the greatest feeling in the world, but both have huge spiritual weights attached to them that often go overlooked until it's too late. Your body needs rest. It does not have the ability to keep up with the Spirit (Mark 6:30-32; Phil.2:25-30). Although you are graced for the called, the body still needs rest.

- Do your part and rest.

- You need help. This has to be one of the biggest failures of pastoring and LEADing, and that's not building other LEADers. Pastors don't understand that church is also a business - a Kingdom business. They have to have the mindset of a pastor and a CEO. It is vitally important to your health and the ministry's growth that you learn how to equip, train LEADers so that you can delegate and LEAD properly. How does this relate to your health? Well, Moses's father-in-law told him that the way he was doing ministry would kill him. He was instructed to find able men to bear the burden with him. Did you hear what the counsel of Jethro told Moses? "Son, you are going to die because you can't operate like you are and expect your mind and body to keep up."

And I'm saying the same thing to you. Whatever trust issues you have, get over it. Learn how and become comfortable with delegation. No miracle or ministry from Jesus came without first having His team. He then gave them power and order. You were never called to be a one-man show. And yes, some are going to fail, come up short, not follow through, etc. Welcome to doing business. Peter failed Jesus, and Jesus didn't get rid of him. Neither did He pick up the pieces. He showed him the error of his ways and made him make the corrections. Boy, I wish I would have had this knowledge. My wife and I have an extensive ministry background. There is not a single department that we haven't either run or worked in. This was our Achilles' heel. Whenever something went wrong, we wouldn't teach, LEAD, or build the person. We would step in and fix it ourselves. The outcome was no growth, members who didn't take on personal accountability as LEADers, and we were the blame. There was no need to believe that members would see and run with the vision if we constantly took it from them. They never took the ownership we believed in because we gave it, but we took it right back by not identifying the correction and allowing them to make the change. And this is why so many LEADers are running rather than LEADing. Hab.2:2 says that your responsibility is to *write the vision and make it plain so that those that read it MAY RUN WITH IT*. Not you!

4. **Define your craft and stay true to it.** You don't have to copy - be an original! There is something unique that you have to offer. Be comfortable with it and trust that it works. God would not have given it to you if not.

5. **Your name means everything!** You are a LEADer; if you fall, the sheep/followers scatter. Protect your calling/purpose. People may try to ruin your reputation, but don't destroy your integrity.

6. **Know you.** How God uniquely crafted you to deliver the Gospel.

7. **Love people/forgive quickly/hold no one guilty and bathe your heart in love.**

8. **Display excellence.** Go over and above. The best at whatever level you are on. Remember, detail makes the difference.

9. **Stay focused on "YOUR ASSIGNMENT."**

10. **Stay in your lane.** Avoid the spirit of competition and comparison, and stay out of the race of hurry (II Cor.10-12-14).

11. **Get out of the way.** LEADers have this proclivity of wanting to do their job and God's job too. You can't do what's God's or carry what's God's.

   - You cannot make the people obey God. Your responsibility is to God; in being accountable to God, you are accountable to the people. This has to be foundational because you must in no wise go beyond God's instructions to the people because God will not break His own laws for you. This is where many LEADers get hurt because they go around God in LEADing the people. This does not mean that Holy Spirit doesn't have the freedom and oversight to change or alter; however, make sure it's Holy Spirit LEADing and not feeling forced.

   - Faith can't go beyond a person's free will, unbelief, or disobedience.

12. **Secure your home and life.** There is a saying on the plane, "Put your mask on first before helping

someone else," and LEADers often leave themselves and their families to suffocate while giving air to everyone else. There will be times of sacrifice, but nothing comes before the wife, kids and you. Think of it like this, God embodied Himself and died for His bride - the church. Yet many LEADers are deceived by the false teaching that the church comes first and leaves their wives to die. God does not expect nor has He called for your home or life to lack or go down while helping others go up.

13. **You NEED Pastoring.** You cannot spend so much time pouring out that you are never poured into yourself. You need to go and sit at the feet of someone with whom you value their anointing, ministry, and life.

14. **Don't allow missed ministry moments to cause you to malfunction.** Jesus tells Peter and *"when you recover, strengthen your brother."* You are going to miss it! Trust me. We all do. Some of us are just afraid to say it. We are often the product of beliefs that we adopt, only to find out later that the theological approach may not have been right. We may say something that doesn't communicate it in the right way. We are not devoid of mistakes. The prophet Samuel missed it at Jesse's house. But it didn't stop him from adjusting and continuing what God had told him to do in selecting the next king. Neither did God strip Him of his title or pull his assignment away. So many times, LEADers stay stuck on mistakes when God has moved on.

Remember this, Number 1: God knew all your flaws and still chose you. This is not to say that we should be comfortable with shortfalls. The point is God didn't say, "I'll wait until you get it together first." He put the gift in an earthen vessel. Number 2: You may make mistakes, but don't allow the mistakes to make you. Repent, pivot and push forward.

15. **Faith and not zeal.** Because it's a good idea doesn't make it a God's idea. If unsure, remember the principle that says there is safety in a multitude of counselors (Proverbs 24:6).

   • Just because it's part of the vision doesn't mean it's for right now. There a time and season to all things under the sun.

16. **Be a Sower.** LEADers should not expect from people what they are unwilling to do themselves. Because we have been commissioned to teach and preach, the Word doesn't exempt us from obeying it ourselves. As LEADers, we are even more responsible for living out the Word of God before the people. We set an example for them to follow. I expect my people to give because I am a giver and I demonstrate it **before them**.

17. **Edit your life.** You have to know what's toxic, and what's good but a distraction when it comes to you; keeping your character and overall spiritual well-being is important. It's not your job to save. It's your job to minister and be a light. It's said that Jesus "hung out" with sinners, but the Bible neither says nor

suggests such. He was there to minister, not to hang with. And that verbiage makes all the difference. **You can't play around with or take for granted the things in life that you should edit, backspace, or delete**.

18. **Live Fasted.** Fasted rather than fasting has become a way of life for me. What often happens is people go on a fast to push things away for a period of time so that they can hear God, get an answer or clarity on something, and even sometimes to correct a life error. They get what they were fasting for - great! But here is the problem. They bring right back into their lives the very things that pushed away or put at a distance the things they were fasting for. What if instead of having times of pushing away, we recognised those things that keep us away and live fasted? It seemed wiser to me that I should get out of God to get into things rather than get out of things to get into God.

From this way of living fasted, I immediately saw how I was overindulging in things, causing my heart's hearing and seeing to become clouded. I immediately realigned and postured my spirit man to stay in alignment with Holy Spirit.

Conclusion
It's About Morals

> But **Daniel purposed in his heart** that he would not defile himself with the portion of the king's meat, nor with the wine which he drank: therefore he requested of the prince of the eunuchs that he might not defile himself.
>
> **Daniel 1:8**

God declared the end from the beginning. This is a powerful scripture and holds all possibilities of victory for any LEADer who understands its depth. This scripture is letting us know that God isn't at work arbitrarily, hoping that things will turn out right. He knows they will turn out right because He planned the end before He started with the beginning. So, how does this relate to morals? Quite simple. Morals are simply standards that a LEADer sets for their lives. Standards are boundaries and guidelines that do not change. They are preset and resolute, so that no matter what comes up, the standard always holds the decision. **The standard determines if it will or will not be done**.

Your standards are the bodyguards of your morals. And if you do not have standards, then your morals rest on the precipice of ruin. Daniel purposed in his heart that he would not defile himself with the portion of the king's table. I believe that he knew what was at stake. His gifts, callings, anointing and possibly his closeness with God weighed on a decision to cling to a standard even if it put his life a stake. Not that he would necessarily lose them, but **the proficiency and accuracy of these things are affected when we disregard morals and are only left operating off skill**. It was their standard that bolstered their ability to stand and yield them a favorable outcome. *And **at the end** of ten days their countenances appeared fairer and fatter in flesh than all the children which did eat the portion of the king's meat.* **16** *Thus Melzar took away the portion of their meat, and the wine that they should drink; and gave them pulse.* **17** *As for these four children, God gave them knowledge and skill in all learning and wisdom: and Daniel had understanding in all visions and dreams,* **19** *And the king communed with them; and among them all was found none like Daniel, Hananiah, Mishael, and Azariah: therefore stood they before the king.* **20 *And in all matters of wisdom and understanding, that the king enquired of them, he found them ten times better than all the magicians and astrologers that were in all his realm*.** (Daniel 1:15-17, 19-20).

LEADer, what are you standing by? What guards you from the appetite of the flesh? What are your non-negotiables? At the time of this writing, Chic-fil-A does not open on Sundays. They are located on some of the busiest strips, in some of the hugest stadiums. When other restaurants are banking on the weekend to put them in the black, this restaurant holds to a standard originated by its founder that on this day we are closed no matter what. There is not anything that has caused them to break this standard. No holiday, no amount of money, and no special person. And because they uphold this standard, on one of the busiest days of the week, when mostly everyone is eating out, they still rank as one of the highest earning and paying fast-food chains in America today. And all over the world, *"my pleasure"* has become an adopted service slogan, even by Fortuune 500 companies..

Do you have standards that are treasured by you as such? Have you even thought of establishing them? That no amount of money, no ungodly advancement by person or power, and no attraction has the power to break, causing collapse to your morals.

Think of Joseph when he was approached by Potiphar's wife. He could have risked it all; may have even gotten away with it. But Joseph's standard was unbreakable and too high. And though it landed him in jail, temporarily, because he remained true to his standards and didn't break morals, he was later promoted to Governor of Egypt. Now imagine, had he broken the barrier of his standards as servant to Potiphar's house and succeeded. What would his moral character have been like as second in charge to Pharoah having full command over all of Egypt?

Protect your morals by acquiring standards that are non-negotiables. All the aforementioned chapters are powerful standards for the life of a LEADer. God is entrusting his people to our care, and I believe that many LEADers have fallen short of their Kingdom duties because they did not establish the right standards from the onset. People should not only be able to trust what LEADers say, LEADers should also have actions that are worth following too. Speaking of Jesus in Mark 7:37 it reads: *And were beyond measure astonished, saying, **He hath done all things well**... We have the ability to have this same testimmony about us, *and to make it your ambition to lead a quiet life: You should mind your own business and work with your hands, just as we told you, 12 so that your daily life may win the respect of outsiders and so that you will not be dependent on anybody* (I Thessalonians 4:11NIV).

Standards are powerful. **Next to Holy Spirit, they are the greatest assets a LEADer can have**. They are the bounds by which we are able to stay true to our moral compass, so that success is not compromised, purpose is achieved, a Kingdom standard is uplifted, and God is glorified.

About the Author

Vincent Robinson and his wife MiShondia pastor Right Way Christian Center Church, in Mobile, Alabama which they founded in 2006. Prior to ministry, Vincent served in the United States Navy and afterwards became an entrepreneur in the hair industry. It was a short time after that Vincent received his call into ministry and God commissioned him to shut down the business and go into ministry full-time. Vincent has worked extensively in ministry from overseeing an extension church, operating a TV Station, to producing his own television ministry broadcast.

Dr. Vincent attended Word of Life Christian College and Theological Smiinary and earned his Doctor of Theology in Ministry from Midwest College of Theology and now serves as founder and president of LEADership Development and Bible Institute in Mobile, AL. In addition, he hosts an annual Kingdom Business Summit empowering the Church in economic evangelism and entrprenuership through Biblical principles. Dr. Vincent is a published author and travels teaching on LEADership, finances, and business. He and his wife MiShondia have 4 children and a grandson.